ENCOUNTERS
WITH THE

Courts Of Heaven

UNAWARE
ENCOUNTERS
WITH THE

Courts Of Heaven

Everyday Occurrences
that Often Go Unnoticed

Emelda Menge Williams

Dedication

With a grateful heart I want to dedicate this book to the Magnificent Trinity:

- To my Daddy God, who loves me and calls me His own
- To Jesus, my Redeemer, my Savior, my Lord, the Lover of my Soul, my Husbandman, and my soon-coming King
- And to Holy Spirit, who leads me and guides me into all truth, He who comforts me and aids me in prayer

Without You in my life, my life would be meaningless, and without You, I would not be where I am today. Thank You for loving me.

Acknowledgements

I want to thank Holy Spirit for placing a spiritual suitcase in my hand with a full itinerary tailored just for me and for bringing me to my vacation destination place called Midbar for a full year and a half, where I found healing and a deeper relationship with Daddy God, Jesus, and with Holy Spirit Himself.

I want to thank Him for introducing Elizabeth A. Nixon's teachings, which gave me my first glance into the courts of Heaven and for Gretchen Mure Rodriguez, who was able to give voice to what I had lived when I had no words to describe it.

I want to thank Him for revealing moments of my life that, in all the years, I had no knowledge that they were connected in a very special way, which one day would lead me to write this book.

I want to thank my husband and my dad for encouraging me in this time of writing and my daughter Abby for her skills that helped me along.

Contents

Foreword by Denise Triche

It's not very often that you read a book like this one, *Unaware Encounters with the Courts of Heaven*. There is no one better qualified to write a book like this about thoughts and life experience than Emelda Williams. As you read through the pages of this book, you will be captivated by the experience of occurrences you might have had or are even now having with your encounters of God as she describes.

Emelda's life demonstrates what she believes. She truly has a heart after God and for His people, and her life story is real. I loved all the scriptures and the principles she placed in her book that supported what she was saying, plus how intimately she speaks about the Magnificent Trinity.

God continually seeks to encourage and uplift His people. Receive and encounter all of God's blessings for your life as you enjoy reading *Unaware Encounters with the Courts of Heaven*.

Denise Triche
FMI Missionary

Introduction

Have you ever had one of those moments when Holy Spirit pops in and says, "Hey, I have something to tell you?" You're not expecting it, but it is wonderful and exciting, and the encounter leaves you invigorated.

At the moment, you are in awe of what is being said, and He unquestionably has your attention, as you sit there trying to comprehend it all, pondering the download of revelation that has just been given. And then the question arises: why has this level of understanding gone unnoticed for so long?

You now realize that the insight given consisted of principles you have operated or participated in for years. But now God is opening your understanding of that participation to another level. You are suddenly seeing it in a fresh and new way. You envision the picture of it in your mind's eye and are taken aback as you perceive what He is saying, suddenly understanding how it all fits together.

Prior to this, you were totally unaware of the bigger picture. Unaware encounters? Courts of Heaven? "What's this all about? And how can this be?" you might ask.

The concept of the courts of Heaven that was given to me consists of two categories. These are realms we operate in, and the two intermingled bring us into a deeper relationship with the Father. I tend to elaborate a little more on the first court in question, for it is vital to the second. I will explain this as we go along.

The first concept of the courts pertains to God's judicial system as we see it in the Scriptures. These principles pertain to all aspects of life, both the now and the eternal. The next concept of the courts pertains to God's wooing us, Him drawing us to Himself. He accomplishes this in various and unusual ways.

What I also received is that there are courts within a court. In chapters to come, I will shed light more thoroughly on this. *Unaware*

Encounters with the Courts of Heaven, when it is all said and done, I would say, is a love story, a love story of redemption and restoration in so many ways. It is my story, but it is also yours—men and women alike.

Again, it is God wooing us, drawing us unto Himself. It is Holy Spirit showing up in the vast areas of life through the Scriptures, saying, "I know where you are and what you're facing, and I have avenues for you to take." He also shows up to provide us with understandings of the legal authority that comes from His Word. It is an authority we can walk in so that we can be overcomers in this life and the life to come, having full assurance that we have access to the realm called the Courts of Heaven and all its wonderful benefits.

The terminology *courts of Heaven*, in the aspect of courtroom activity may be foreign to you as it was to me. But from the beginning of time, I can assure you that angels have interacted with this realm, and so have men and women. The activity of this realm is recorded from Genesis to Revelation.

You would think that if we had encounters with this realm—the courts of Heaven and its principles—we would know it, right? Sometimes that is the case, but not always. It may be a lack of knowledge or it may be an area we have not yet discovered because this particular revelation of God's Word has not yet come to us.

Strangely enough, looking back to when I first started my walk with the Lord, I tended to gravitate toward biblical principles of courtroom activity without placing them in an actual courtroom setting, much less in a heavenly setting. That was not what I envisioned. In fact, I didn't envision anything at all, although I somehow knew inwardly that these principles were real. For a lengthy period, I had been having an inward witness. I was adamant about these principles and would speak of them quite often. I knew that God upheld them, for it was the truth of His Word.

So let's stop for a moment. Just from what you have read so far, I hope I'm sparking something within you that may cause you to recall moments in your own life, moments when you utilized God's Word and it connected you to His principles and with the courts of Heaven.

Moving forward in my own life, I came to realize, as Holy Spirit revealed, that I only saw in part, and I only understood in part concerning this topic. I did not yet realize the magnitude of it all. If I had, I am most certain I would have given myself to the study of it much earlier. I'm sure you have seen yourself standing in this same place concerning the Word of God in some area or other of life.

Our "unawareness" explains how and why we can read the Word of God day in and day out but not perceive the depth of it on a given matter. This was true of myself, although I had been born again for forty-two years and, without a doubt, knew I'd had several encounters with Daddy God, Jesus, and Holy Spirit. I'm sure you can say the same.

In fact, I'm just now seeing angles or facets of the concept of having unaware encounters that connect to what is being called the courts of Heaven and its principles. Sometimes in life, we are expecting big, bold aha moments when we hear, "Thus saith the Lord" and can then declare, "I had an encounter with God!" But all along, we have been connecting with God in the simplest of ways.

As believers in Christ Jesus, our spirit man has been awakened to the principles and standards of the living God. Therefore, our spirit man is in perfect alignment with Him. But, as the Scriptures say, our mind needs to be renewed daily. My spirit knew exactly what was being said when Holy Spirit spoke. I had an inner witness, but how blind of me that for so many years I had not seen it in its entirety.

> *The unfolding of your words gives light;*
> *it gives understanding to the simple.*
> Psalm 119:130

> *That the God of our Lord Jesus Christ,*
> *the Father of glory, may give unto you*

the spirit of wisdom and revelation in the knowledge of him: the eyes of your understanding being enlightened; that ye may know what is the hope of his calling, and what the riches of the glory of his inheritance in the saints.

Ephesians 1:17-18, KJV

Open my eyes that I may see wonderful things in your law.

Psalm 119:18

God's manifold wisdom is beyond measure, and we cannot comprehend it all at once. He has appointed times when He unfolds and reveals truths, whereby we can grow and mature in the knowledge of His Word. He delivers these truths by way of various avenues that we can relate to.

As believers, the most important attribute we can have is to remain teachable. God's Word is alive and active, and it is eternally producing. The revelation of His Word can reflect beautiful marks on our lives, showing that we have been in His presence, and by these we can truly say we have interacted and have had encounters with Him in our everyday life. The amazing thing is that these encounters come in the simplest ways we could ever imagine. That is what Holy Spirit did for me, and that is what He wants to do for you too.

On my journey, He gave me understanding of different events and situations of my past and present that somehow connected me to the activity in the heavenly realm and the protocols of God's legal system, principles of the courts which are based on God's governmental standards. This is not something new; it has always been, and we have all been partaking of it, to some degree, whether we are aware of it or not.

If you have studied the courts of Heaven, you know that is where we earthlings access God, who is in Heaven. He showed me that with several of my encounters, it was not that I went before God for an encounter, but that He, from His court, came and encountered me. This is part of the wooing I am referring to. These were times when He came to bless me in peculiar ways. Can you relate? I know you can.

With several of the encounters, verdicts and rulings from these principles of the courts were put into motion, accusations from the accuser were silenced, and I found favor with God. I will explain this in the coming chapters and how I was made aware of these principles, as Holy Spirit led me step by step on this journey.

I am a person who loves visuals. A picture is worth a thousand words. Well, maybe not a thousand, but you get the gist of what I'm implying. In general, people respond to and retain more from seeing pictures better than words alone. In a picture, you can see what is being said. Holy Spirit, knowing all too well my love for visuals, gave me a teaching tool to use that demonstrates God's governmental standards. It is vital for you to comprehend and see for yourself that there is a legal realm streaming throughout the Word of God.

Due to my own experience, there were barriers that prohibited me from receiving understanding on the abundance of court activity in the Word. These barriers were 1). Lacking to see—no spiritual insight to biblical truths concerning the courts of Heaven. 2.) Running over words—not giving thought. 3.) Protocols—God's ways of legal activity in His Word.

I feel it is relevant to part of my journey that I elaborate on a few scriptures on this subject. I want to begin by painting a picture in your mind's eye through the lens of scriptures of a spiritual government and who presides there.

As you continue to read, the picture will become more clear, and when it is all said and done, you will see yourself connecting with this realm. You will see how you have been operating in the principles of the courts on several layers that pertains to your faith. From salvation to worshipping to intercession and more, your relationship with the Word will be brought to new heights.

I will begin with a picture of Him who upholds this governmental system. Take your time with each scripture. Don't run through them. Close your eyes and envision what you are reading. Let this picture begin to take form on the canvas of your mind's eye. As you do, Holy Spirit will confirm the Word of this realm to you, and He will give you understanding. You will begin seeing from the Word where such activity is recorded:

God is a righteous judge.   Psalm 7:11

All rise! For God now comes to judge as He convenes heaven's courtroom.
Psalm 82:1, TPT

I watched till thrones were put in place,
And the Ancient of Days was seated;
His garment was white as snow,
And the hair of His head was like pure wool.
His throne was a fiery flame,
Its wheels a burning fire;
A fiery stream issued and came forth from before Him.
A thousand thousands ministered to Him;
Ten thousand times ten thousands stood before Him.

The court was seated,
And the books were opened.

Daniel 7:9-10, NKJV

This is what we see happening in an earthly courtroom when the judge comes in and we watch him take his seat, and then suddenly court is in session.

Righteousness and justice are the foundation of your throne;
love and faithfulness go before you.

Psalm 89:14

For the LORD your God is God of gods and LORD of lords, the great God, mighty and awesome, who shows no partiality and accepts no bribes.

Deuteronomy 10:17

For the LORD is righteous,
he loves justice.   Psalm 11:7
Put me in remembrance;
Let us contend together;

State your case, that you may be acquit-
ted. Isaiah 43:26, NKJV

Are you beginning to see this heavenly courtroom setting in your mind's eye from these scriptures? If so, I'm sure it is beginning to capture your attention, and you're wanting to see more. Let us get this picture painted and see how we have all been *Operating in the Courts of Heaven Unaware.*

Don't be afraid, my dear friend, about going into the courts of the Lord. Naturally speaking, who wants to be summoned to court, right, especially if you know you are guilty? But don't be afraid. God is waiting for you, and He is in on your side.

Coming into the courts does not mean that something is always against you. It can mean that there is something great and glorious just waiting for you.

Emelda Menge Williams
Houma, Louisiana

CHAPTER 1

Awakening to Unaware Encounters with the Courts of Heaven

Welcome to the unaware encounters that connected me to what are called the courts of Heaven. I am not afraid to make this bold statement: You, too, have had unaware experiences operating in the principles of this realm.

My surprise visitation with this revelation took place at the beginning of January 2022. At this writing, I am sixty-four years old and been saved for forty-two of those years, and yet here I was learning new principles from God's Word! I have come to a great understanding that the more I learn about the Word of God, the more I see just how little I know.

My visitation took place on a chilly January day. I was sewing on a quilt for a friend of mine, and while doing so, I heard the still small voice within me saying, "You have had many encounters with the courts of Heaven in your lifetime. Let me show you." I quickly grabbed my pen and some paper and began writing, as Holy Spirit relayed each encounter. As He did so, I found myself in a state of awe, for I was able to recall each one and, therefore, was able to perceive what He was saying.

The reason I was able to understand was due to the fact that Holy Spirit had placed teachings on this subject in front of me two years before this. Because I was captivated by it, it had my attention, and I was compelled to study on this subject of the courts of Heaven, and I did this for some time.

Now, there is a principle that's set in motion, whether you apply it for the good or the bad. It is: "Whatever we make room for, we will get more of." That was what happened in my case. I made room for this teaching of God's Word in my life, and as time went by, I came to understand more and more on the subject. This gave substance for Holy Spirit to interact with me based on the knowledge I had received. If I had not studied this subject, I would not have been able to accept what He was now showing me. I would not have been able to receive what He wanted to tell me concerning my encounters with the courts. And, consequently, I would have missed out on a blessing because it would have been a foreign subject as far as I was concerned.

Since I had given myself to the study of this teaching, Holy Spirit was able to breathe more life on the matter, and it became personal to me. I was not taking on something I had only read about from someone else.

As I look back on that day I was sewing, two of the fabrics I used in the quilting now speak volumes to me. It's funny how things work out. One fabric had swirls of vibrant colors throughout. Understanding spiritual concepts, we know that whirlwinds swirling can be a sign of an opened portal from Heaven. It just so happened, that a heavenly portal was opened over me that day.

The other pattern was an array of multicolored butterflies. Spiritually, butterflies are a sign of new birth. What a combination of fabrics! God had opened a portal, giving me new insights to understand these unaware encounters I had been having that somehow connected with the courts of Heaven, God's governmental realm, His principles, and more.

I can't claim any bragging rights. I was not raised in a born-again, Spirit-filled home, where I would have been introduced to the things of God as I have since come to know them. I was the first generation in my family to experience the salvation of God. The phrases *heavenly encounters* or *courts of Heaven* were not words spoken around me when I was young.

I did have a limited knowledge of God in my upbringing. My grandmother made sure of that. On Sundays, the first thing she asked when we walked into her home was, "Did you all go to church this morning?" No one got under her radar. Yes, I went to church, and I did get to know ABOUT God and His Son, Jesus. Sad to say, I knew very little of Holy Spirit. I was told I had received Him when they slapped my face during my Confirmation.

In all reality, I did not know God, Jesus, or Holy Spirit personally, and getting to know them personally is the key to having a relationship with the Trinity. That, I definitely did not have. It was a certainty that I had absolutely no knowledge concerning the courts of Heaven. That was nowhere in my sights.

What I can say is this: when I was a child, I began to sense that I was guilty of something. I would pray the Our Father and the Act of Contrition. Those prayers, or petitions, before God were all I knew. I can assure you that I had no insight that when I prayed those prayers or petitions, they were intended to be presented before a heavenly court system.

I am very grateful for the limited knowledge I was given as a child. It was a small measure, but I was taught to believe in God and know that there was a God. In the light of eternity, that was huge. I could have ended up in an atheistic family and believed that God didn't even exist. Thank God, that wasn't the case.

But whether you were born into a family with a knowledge of God or not, Holy Spirit is more than able to open your eyes to the truth of God's Word. And He is longing to do just that for you.

Coming back to the encounters: Prior to this sudden awareness that was being made known to me, before I gave Jesus my life as an adult, the only heavenly encounter that stood out came from the Christmas story. It was when the angel spoke to Mary, saying that she would bear the Son of God. In response, she acknowledged, *"Let it be to me according to your word"* (Luke 1:38, NKJV). This encounter became a legal agreement—God's spoken words to her and her words back to Him. It was an encounter that forever marked Mary's life.

The thing that stood out to me is that Mary was not on her knees petitioning God for anything at that moment. She was just going about her day like she normally would have, when God decided to interact with her from His courts by way of an angel. The angel spoke something directly to Mary, she came into agreement with what was being said, and it became a legal contract which came to flourishing.

This was one of the concepts Holy Spirit wanted me to see concerning some of the encounters I had experienced. Some encounters didn't occur because I was kneeling in prayer, accessing Heaven in those moments. As with Mary, I was just going about my daily activities. Somehow and some way, Holy Spirit would show up to guide me or encourage me or just to bless me in peculiar ways. These were significant moments that also marked my life.

The other concept Holy Spirit opened to me was this: There were times when I did pray, and those prayers connected to the principles of the courts. Many times, these encounters related to some form of legal activity concerning the Word of God for my life or my family. I was heading in the right direction but operating unknowingly as far as terminology was concerned. I would have just said that I was coming into God's presence, which was true. But now I was being shown a broader aspect of coming into His presence. There was much more activity taking place than I had realized. Being still blind to the subject, I didn't yet see myself in a courtroom or see myself presenting my petition in the dimension or realm of a court.

I was not ignorant concerning prayer. I had heard many messages and read lots of books on that subject. I became familiar with prayers of supplication, intercessory prayers, prayers of thanksgiving, prayers of praise, prayers of binding and loosing, and the list can go on. But I had never heard of praying before the courts of Heaven. This was new to me.

I had read Psalm 100:4 (KJV):

Enter into his gates with thanksgiving, and into his courts with praise.

Yes, I had sung about a court where I could go to thank God, praise Him, and worship

Him. I sang that psalm many times, but I still failed to understand the fullness of it.

God has a wonderful sense of humor. About two years into being born again, I spent a whole summer and a whole winter under a tent studying with our congregation on the subject " The Tabernacle of Moses." It was a fabulous study, even though it was a hot summer and a very cold winter. This just goes to show that you can have an extensive study of the inner and outer courts and yet not perceive the particular nugget Holy Spirit wants to reveal.

I have come to learn from the Word of God that there are dimensions, or realms, of Heaven where other courts preside for our welfare and that of others, dimensions where we access God as our Father, our Friend, and yes, even as our Judge. We have all accessed these realms, but I, for one, did not understand the fullness of how they worked.

As you read this book, I pray that Holy Spirit will bring to your remembrance the many encounters you have had, even down to those that may seem to have been very small. Still, they were heavenly encounters you had, and in one way or another, they somehow connected you with the courts of Heaven. You will be amazed to see, as you continue to read, that this has been going on daily since you have given your life to Jesus. Walk with me now, as Holy Spirit unfolds to us these unaware encounters.

CHAPTER 2

Heaven and Earth: Mirror Images

My introduction to the courts of Heaven began in 2019. At the time, I was hosting a Bible study in my home, teaching on Psalm 91. During this period, Holy Spirit drew me away a time or two. He then introduced me to a woman named Elizabeth Nixon. I had never heard of her, but she was teaching on what she called "The Courts of Heaven."

Mrs. Nixon was a renowned attorney who practiced law before the United States Supreme Court. Being born-again and Spirit-filled, her profession led her to examine the Word of God with a whole different perspective. As she studied the Word, she began to see a pattern between the way God governed and the way earth governed its court matters. The conclusion of her findings revealed that earth's judicial systems mirror what the Bible says. They are parallel to God's judicial system.

Holy Spirit, as I said earlier, had a way of putting such teachings in front of me, and I knew that I needed to give heed to them. Although I knew I needed to stay on course and remain faithful to my Bible study, this teaching was always at the back of my mind. I had tasted, and I wanted more.

After I completed the study on Psalm 91, Holy Spirit brought me back to this subject of "The Courts of Heaven." He propelled me forward and had me diving deep into this new-found study (which proved not to be new after all).

God is the Supreme Judge, and He presides over His courts, which are in Heaven. Just as earthly courts have different divisions to accommodate a variety of needs, so do Heaven's courts. The Word of God may not present us with an actual name for each court, but, in all reality, they're there. We simply have not envisioned them as such.

The way I see the courts of Heaven is simple: We have access to various spiritual courts. They are revealed by the principles coming from the Word of God. We take these principles, or laws, build cases according to our need, and present them before the heavenly court.

I can now see so much of my Christian experience in the light of courtroom activity. This is where verdicts are rendered and needs are met pertaining to all the various areas of our lives.

I now see my prayer in a new dimension. As I pray, I can envision the activity taking place in Heaven's courts. If my need requires a lawyer, I envision Jesus defending me against the prosecutor, who is Satan, and the judge is none other than God Himself. He will always rule in my favor. In other words, my prayers have a landing place.

Since becoming a believer, I have always prayed, and I have always envisioned God receiving my prayers because of the finished work of Jesus. But this nugget Holy Spirit revealed to me takes my prayers to the next level.

In the coming chapters, I will name a few of the courts I have visited and expound on them from the Word of God. They mirror the courts in the earthly realm, and you will easily see the similarities between the two.

Since I am on the subject of how God mirrors earth to Heaven concerning the courts, I feel led to touch base on two other topics that come under the same heading. We can see that God is consistent throughout His Word on all matters. This mirroring is not limited to the courts or legal issues. We can see a case has already been established pertaining to mirroring by the Word on other subjects as well.

Take, for instance, like the word faith. It has been mentioned from the beginning of time. We read of many, like Abraham, who was seen as the father of faith. We know that he stepped out in faith, and that pleased God. But at a specific time in history, God unfolded deeper principles of the Word of faith to His people. It was principles to teach one how to operate in faith on a higher level.

I was not around for the beginning of this revelation which God unfolded to a man by the name of Evangelist E.W. Kenyon. He was active back in the late 1930s and 40s, and I didn't come along until the late 50s. God continued to reveal more of the word of faith message to Kenneth Hagin in the 1980s, and that was where I started my walk with the Lord.

So how does operating in this "word of faith," mirror Heaven? If we are children who now belong to God, who operates by faith in Heaven. Therefore, we, too, are called to operate by faith here on earth according to the Scriptures. Why? Because we are made in His image. We see God speaking by faith, calling forth from Heaven substance to the earth. We are to speak by faith, calling forth from earth to Heaven for substances.

In the Scriptures we read:

In the beginning God created the Heaven and the earth. Now the earth was formless and empty, darkness was over the surface of the deep, and the Spirit of God was hovering over the waters. And God said, "Let there be light," and there was light.   Genesis 1:1-3

Now faith is the substance of things hoped for, the evidence of things not seen.   Hebrews 11:1, KJV

For therein is the righteousness of God revealed from faith to faith: as it is written, The just shall live by faith.
                    Romans 1:17, KJV

Truly I tell you, if anyone says to this mountain, "Go, throw yourself into the sea," and does not doubt in their heart but believes that what they say will happen, it will be done for them.
                    Mark 11:23

The other topic I felt to unfold that mirrors Heaven concerns angels. It is not that we have not heard about angels. We were always told as children that we had a guardian angel watching over us. I feel that, for myself, growing up, that concept came from a religious mindset. It was not due to having a personal encounter with any angels. From early on, I can recall a picture my grandmother had on her wall. It entailed a stream flowing with a small bridge crossing over it. On the bridge were two children walking, and there, in their presence, was the guardian angel at their sides, protecting them. I'm sure you have also seen this same picture at some time. Did it ever cross your mind that this was truly possible, that we can have interactions with angels here and now just as Heaven interacts with them there?

In recent years, God is revealing to us deeper layers of knowledge about angels. Angels are not only for Heaven's use. In the Scriptures we see God giving assignments to angels to intervene on behalf of various individuals. In turn, through the Scriptures, we are given instructions for having angels intervene on our behalf here on earth.

Praise the LORD, *you His angels,*
you mighty ones who do His bidding,
who obey His word.   Psalm 103:20

Are not all angels ministering spirits
sent to serve those who will inherit sal-
vation?   Hebrews 1:14

We have had the honor of the well-known minister named Joshua Mills coming to minister on angels in our services. Through the knowledge coming forth from his books and CDs, I have come to know how to activate and know my angel's name. How awesome is that?

You may question, "Why would God allow us to know the name of our angel or even why they were sent to us?" At times He does.

That teaching brought me into an encounter with an angel. I didn't see her, but she made her presence known to me twice. One evening, as I was listening to the activation message, I joined in the prayer Joshua was releasing for the angel's name to come forth.

After I prayed, a word came to me, but it was so glorious that I dismissed it.

Two days later, I was listening to the same message while I was cooking, and I repeated the prayer again. The only difference this time was that I didn't ask for the name to be revealed. This time, I said, "I thank You for the release of my angel's name." Why did I do that? Because I had already asked, so now it was time to give thanks.

At that very moment, coming from the right side of me, I heard the same word as before, and it was very clear and precise. I was taken by it. I stopped in my tracks, stopped doing what I was doing, and I literally turned my face to the right because I felt the presence of my angel. It was as if she should have been in bodily form; it was just that real. I looked into her face in the spirit realm and said so profoundly, "REALLY! THAT'S YOUR NAME, SPLENDOR?" SPLENDOR it was.

Within the next few days, God confirmed this visitation to me, and He did it by way of me scrolling through Pinterest. He can use whatever means He wants to get our attention, and that He did.

My eyes locked onto an advertisement of what I thought had something to do with Shabby Chic designs. My home décor is just that. So, with that, what I thought was a Shabby Chic article, I preceded to expand on the photo, and this's what it said: "Garments of splendor, covered by grace, clothed in freedom." The only word that was in big bold letters was **SPLENDOR**. I would have to say that was God letting me know that I had heard right. That was my angel's name!

In the Scriptures we can read about angels such as Gabriel and Michael, along with their functions.

On my journey with the courts, Elizabeth Nixon was the only person I had heard of who spoke on this subject, and it was through her that I was able to comprehend the mirroring of the courts. I felt it would be wise on my part to search out other seasoned ministers who were teaching on this subject as well. I wanted to hear these truths out of the mouths of two or three, or even four or five.

However, I had also learned early on that we need to search things out for ourselves, and I did. Believe me, I was on a hunt. In my searching, I found someone I was familiar with, and he had a couple of messages, and I was able to obtain one of them quite easily.

The other message, for some reason, was not offered on his web site. I called his office and inquired about it. The person on the other end said, "Oh, yes, we have that, but it's a classic from the vault." This message was from a 2003 conference.

I can tell you right now it did not matter what conference it came from. I wanted it, and I bought the complete six-pack DVD set, even though only one of the messages pertained to the matters of the courts. Now I had it, and it was an eye-opener on this subject.

When I got to thinking about it, I was amazed that this message had been going forth since 2003, it was now considered a classic, and I was just receiving insight on it nineteen years later.

It was amazing to look back on all the years of reading and studying the Word and hearing ministers preach it, and yet I had never heard of the concept or even the terminology of the courts of Heaven. It has been wonderful to hear from the different ministers Holy Spirit has led me to. That journey, in itself, has been exhilarating. He led me from one person to another because it was opening to me a whole new realm.

It is important for each of us to keep in mind that God has not given all there is to know to just one person. But the knowledge He gives one concerning any subject will usually intersect with someone else's revelation. The beauty of it all is that they are all in sync, and we get the benefit of each one's nugget or nuggets. This is how God works. We get to glean from several, and the knowledge we glean makes up the whole.

Let me take it a step further. The people God leads us to may not be in our inner circle of affiliation, and yet it is in our best interests not to become closed-minded to them. Having the mindset that it is only our four and no more with the knowledge of the Word of God is not healthy. If I had been close-minded, I would have missed out on many blessings.

It is a funny thing. When we want to buy a new car, we pick a style we like, and what happens next? Everywhere we go, we seem to see them. We had not realized there were so many of them out there. It was the same with the teachings on the courts of Heaven.

As I gave myself to these teachings, I began seeing this message everywhere. Not just from the resources Holy Spirit led me to or those I obtained on my own. My ears were wide open, and that was all I was hearing. All I know is that I dove in and purchased lots of material on the subject. I was captivated. Not long after that, I began to envision the whole court scenario. It was very exciting.

As a side note, this is something to think about: We are all anticipating going to Heaven, myself included. We cannot wait to get there. But with all things considered, we are not staying there. One day we will be coming back to rule and reign with God here on earth from the New Jerusalem.

So, keep in mind the way God governs Heaven, for it will be the same way He governs when He comes back here. It will be no different than He does now. Why would He want to change His principles concerning government? He won't. He doesn't change.

With that in mind, let us lay a foundation of earth mirroring Heaven by looking at various scriptures on this matter. Within these scriptures you will recognize legal terms that are also used in our judicial system. These words come from my own study notes with their Hebrew or Greek meanings. Getting to the root of these words enables us to comprehend what is really being said in the Scriptures.

Let us continue to lay this foundation by painting this courtroom concept in your mind's eye, as we stroke this canvas with words from various scriptures that pertain to the courts of Heaven. In so doing, you will be able to relate to my unaware encounters as Holy Spirit revealed them to me.

Put me in remembrance,
Let us contend together,
State your case, that you may be
acquitted.   Isaiah 43:26, NKJV
                    (Emphasis Mine)

The word *acquitted,* according to the *Merriam-Webster Dictionary,* means "to discharge completely (as from an accusation or obligation)." It also means "to vindicate."

The thesaurus expansion of the word *acquit* is: "To free from a charge of wrong doing. To redeem."

In these two verses alone, we see that God is speaking from Heaven as a judge would speak to one from an earthly court setting. I am hoping you are beginning to see that there is a mirroring of Heaven to earth.

The Courts of God

I watched till thrones were put in place,
And the Ancient of Days was seated;
His garment was white as snow,
And the hair of His head was like pure wool,

49

His throne was a fiery flame,
Its wheels a burning fire;
A fiery stream issued
And came forth from before Him.
A thousand thousands ministered to Him;
Ten thousand times ten thousand stood before Him.
The court was seated,
And the books were opened.

Daniel 7:9-10, NKJV
(Emphasis Mine)

*God **presides** in the great assembly* *[***courts***];*
*he **renders judgement** among the "gods."* Psalm 82:1
(Emphasis Mine)

*And as it is appointed unto men once to die, but after this the **judgment**.*

Hebrews 9:27, KJV
(Emphasis Mine)

50

God: *(Bible Tools Greek/Hebrew Definitions Strong's #2316:Theos. Thayer's Greek Lexicon 4a1):* **Magistrate** or **Divine Judge**:

> *There is* **one lawgiver,** *who is able to save and to destroy.* James 4:12, KJV
> (Emphasis Mine)

> *God* **judgeth** *the righteous, and God is angry with the wicked every day.*
> Psalm 7:11, KJV
> (Emphasis Mine)

Judge: *Bible Tool Greek/Hebrew Definitions, Strong's Concordance #8199: shaphat,* **"to judge,** to govern." *Brown-Driver-Briggs Hebrew Lexicon*: "1) to judge, govern, vindicate, punish, 1a2) to decide controversy (of God, man)."

> *But you have come to Mount Zion, to the city of the living God, the heavenly Jerusalem. You have come to thousands upon thousands of angles in joyful assembly, to the church of the firstborn, whose names*

are written in heaven. You have come to **_God, the Judge_** *of all, to the spirits of the righteous made perfect, to Jesus the* **_mediator_** *of a new covenant, and to the sprinkled blood that speaks better word than the blood of Abel.* Hebrews 12:22-24
(Emphasis Mine)

And the Lord said, "Listen to what the unjust judge says. And will not God bring about **_justice_** *for his chosen, who cry out to him day and night? Will he keep putting them off? I tell you; he will see that they get* **_justice_** *and quickly."* Luke 18:6-8
(Emphasis Mine)

Lawgiver: *Strong's Concordance* #3550: *nomothetes,* **"a lawgiver."** *Strong's Hebrew* #2710: *chaqaq. Outline of Bible Usage:* **"one who decrees, lawgiver."**

For the Lord *is our* **_judge_**, *the* Lord *is our* **_lawgiver_**, *the* Lord *is our king: he will save us.* Isaiah 33:22, KJV
(Emphasis Mine)

JESUS, OUR DEFENDING ATTORNEY:

Jesus — Our *Mediator/Arbitrator*

Biblehub.com, *Strong's* Greek #3315: *mesiteuo*, "to interpose, mediate." *Thayer's Greek Lexicon*: "1. **To act as a mediator**, between litigating or covenanting parties 1a) to accomplish something by interposing between two parties." *Strong's Exhaustive Concordance*: from *mesites*, "to interpose (as arbiter)."

> *For there is [only] one God and [only] one **Mediator** between God and mankind, the Man Christ Jesus.*
> 1 Timothy 2:5, AMP
> (Emphasis Mine)

Jesus — Our Advocate/Defense Lawyer/ Attorney

Bible Tool Greek/Hebrew Definitions Strong's Concordance #3875: *parakletos* "an intercessor, consoler, **advocate**, comforter." *Thayer's Greek Lexicon*: "1) summoned, called to one's side, especially called to one's aid. 1a) one who pleads another's cause before a judge, a pleader, counsel for defense, legal assistant, an **advocate,** 1b1) of Christ in His exaltation at God's right hand, pleading with God the Father for the pardon of our sins."

> *My little children, these things I write unto you, that you sin not. And if any man sin, we have an* **<u>advocate</u>** *with the Father, Jesus Christ the righteous.*
>
> 1 John 2:1, KJV
> (Emphasis Mine)

ON EARTH, WE HAVE THE PARACLETE, HOLY SPIRIT, AND IN HEAVEN, THE PARACLETE, JESUS!

Satan—the Prosecuting Attorney:

Accuser – *Bible Tool Greek/Hebrew Strong's* #2723: *kategoreo,* #2725: "to be a plaintiff, i.e. to charge with some offense: accuse, object." *Thayer's Greek Lexicon*: "1) to accuse 1a) before a judge to make an accusation 1b) of an extra-judicial accusation."

Liddell-Scott-Jones Definitions: "accuser, public prosecutor."

> *And I heard a loud voice saying in heaven, Now is come salvation, and strength, and the kingdom of God, and the power of his Christ: for the **accuser** of the breather is cast down, which **accused** them before God, day and night.*
>
> Revelation 12:10, KJV
> (Emphasis Mine)

> *Now there was a day when the sons of God came to present themselves before the Lord, and Satan came also among them. And the Lord said unto Satan, Whence comest thou?*
> *Then Satan answered the Lord, and said, From going to and fro in the earth, and from walking up and down in it.*
> *And the Lord said unto Satan, Hast thou considered my servant Job, that there is none like him in the earth, a perfect and an upright man, one that feareth God, and eschewed evil?*

Then Satan answered the LORD, *and said,* <u>*Doth Job fear God for nought?*</u> <u>*Hast not thou made an hedge about him,*</u> <u>*and about his house, and about all that*</u> <u>*he hath on every side? thou hast blessed*</u> <u>*the work of his hands, and his substance*</u> <u>*is increased in the land. But put forth*</u> <u>*thine hand now, and touch all that he*</u> <u>*hath, and he will curse thee to thy face.*</u>

Job 1:6-12, KJV

(Emphasis Mine)

ADVERSARY – *Bible Tool Strong's Greek* #476: *antidikos,* "**an opponent, adversary** in a **lawsuit.**"

"Be sober, be vigilant; because your **<u>adversary the devil</u>***, as a roaring lion, walketh about, seeking whom he may devour.*   1 Peter 5:8, KJV

(Emphasis Mine)

Petitions — *Bible Tool Greek/Hebrew Definitions, Strong's Concordance* #7596: *shelah,* "a **petition**, request." *Brown-Driver-Briggs*

Hebrew Lexicon: "1) request, thing asked for, demand, 1a) request, **petition.**"

> *And this is the confidence that we have in him, that, if we ask any thing according to his will, he heareth us, and if we know that he hears us, whatsoever we ask, we know that we have the **petitions** that we desired of him.*
>
> 1 John 5:14-15, KJV
> (Emphasis Mine)

> *I urge, then, first of all that **petitions**, prayers, intercession and thanksgiving be made for all people.* 1 Timothy 2:1
> (Emphasis Mine)

> *We will rejoice in thy salvation, and in the name of our God we will set up our banners: the* Lord *fulfill all thy **petitions**.* Psalm 20:5, KJV
> (Emphasis Mine)

> *Do not be anxious about anything, but in every situation, by prayer and **peti-***

__tion__, with thanksgiving, present your requests to God.   Philippians 4:6
(Emphasis Mine)

The Persecutors:

LORD, I have so many __persecutors__! Many are rising up against me!
     Psalm 3:1, ISV
(Emphasis Mine)

The Verdict:

A divine __verdict__ is on the lips of the king;
His mouth should not err in __judgment__.   Proverbs 16:10, NASB
(Emphasis Mine)

The Sentence:

And Pilate gave __sentence__ that it should be as they required.   Luke 23:24, KJV
(Emphasis Mine)

As I was studying this topic, Holy Spirit made me aware of another simple truth that pertains to the courts. It is where I had acknowledged God in the realms as Father, Friend, and Judge during my journey, but once again, was unaware of the bigger picture when it came down to it. As I said, these realms are seen in the Scriptures—Father, Friend, and Judge.

The First Realm, Father

> *One of His disciples said to Him, "Lord teach us to pray, as John also taught his disciples."*
> *So He said to them, "When you pray, say:*
>
> *Our Father in heaven,*
> *Hallowed be Your name.*
> *Your kingdom come.*
> *Your will be done*
> *On earth as it is in heaven.*
> *Give us each day by day our daily bread."* Luke 11:1-3, NKJV

This realm is entering the court when we come to our Father for our personal needs or for our families. Hebrews 4:16 (NKJV) tells us about this court:

> *Let us therefore come boldly to the* <u>*throne of grace*</u>*, that we may obtain mercy and find grace to help in time of need.* (Emphasis Mine)

The Second Realm, Friend

This was a time when Jesus painted a picture in the mind's eye of His listeners, while He told this story:

> *And He said to them, "Which of you shall have a friend, and go to him at midnight and say to him, 'Friend, lend me three loaves; for a friend of mine has to come to me on his journey, and I have nothing to set before him'; and he will answer from within and say, 'Do not trouble me; the door is now shut, and my children are with me in bed; I cannot rise and give to*

you'? I say to you, though he will not rise and give to him because he is his friend, yet because of his persistence he will rise and give him as many as he needs."

Luke 11:5-8, NKJV

This is a time when we come before God as our Friend in prayer on behalf of another friend, a family member, or whoever He lays on our heart who needs prayer. This is intercession. It is standing in the gap for another.

The Third Realm, Judge

This also was a time when Jesus painted a picture in the mind's eye of His listeners, while He told this story:

Then He spoke a parable to them, that men always ought to pray and not lose heart, saying: "There was a certain man in a city a judge who did not fear God nor regard man. Now there was a widow in the city; and she came to him, saying, 'Get justice for me from my adversary.'

61

And he would not for a while; but afterward he said within himself, 'Though I do not fear God nor regard man, yet because this widow troubles me I will avenge her, lest by her continual coming she weary me."

Then the Lord said, "Hear what the unjust judge said. And shall God not avenge His own elect who cry out day and night to Him, though He bears long with them? I tell you that He will avenge them speedily." Luke 18:1-8, NKJV

One of the reasons we enter this court is that when we see the need to receive Jesus as our own personal Lord and Savior, we need God to clear us of the penalty of sin so that we can become a child of Almighty God.

There is another time to come into this court. It is when Satan has an accusation against us after we are born again. When we come before God as Judge, we need a defense lawyer to plead our case. We enter this court when the enemy has a legal right to stop our prayers.

Sometimes we wonder why our prayers are not being answered. By the words we speak, we give the enemy legal rights to hinder the answers from coming. We begin to question why the delay. Is it that God does not love me enough? What's the hold-up? Without having the understanding of why it is taking so long, it can become frustrating, to say the least.

When Holy Spirit reveals what the problem is, if it is coming from us, we can go make it right with God by repenting and then God will revoke the accusation. He will issue a restraining order and silence the accuser. In this way, He will render a ruling in our favor because we have come before His court with this matter.

Let me encourage you that as you read the Word of God, begin underlining legal terms. This will broaden your understanding of God's governmental principles, and this will be beneficial for your prayer life.

What I am sharing here is only to give you a basic understanding in case you were not aware of this concept. As a reminder, I want to reiterate that most of my encounters deal with this side of the courts. I hope you are beginning to get the picture, the visual in your mind's eye. This way you will be able to relate with the encounters. And you will also begin to understand better your own encounters, as Holy Spirit reveals them to you.

When that still, small voice came, I was not thinking on this subject at all. My focus was fixed on the quilt I was making that day. In my own words, I was "minding my own business" when Holy Spirit said, "Hey, let me show you how you've been operating in the courts of Heaven unaware."

My First Unaware Encounter
(A Verdict, Not Guilty)

It was the middle of December 1979, and I was driving home from the grocery store. As I was making my way back, I heard a loud thump against the van I was driving. It caught my attention, and I quickly made my way to the shoulder of the road.

As soon as the van stopped, I opened my door and began looking around, questioning what had just taken place. I was puzzled because there was nothing in my view that could have caused that loud thump.

I began examining the front as well as the sides of the vehicle, but there was no evidence of anything wrong. I proceeded to the back of the van, and again there was nothing wrong or out of place.

I then did what anyone else would have done. I bent over and looked underneath the vehicle. To my horror, I could not believe what my eyes caught sight of. Although it seemed like a blur at the moment, it was a nightmare in the making. My eyes locked onto the body of a small child.

The body was pressed up against the back axel with its back toward me, preventing me from seeing what the gender of the child was. I was stunned because I had not been expecting that. No way! No how! What a shock, to say the least. It was mortifying, and I pretty much lost it at that moment. I remember jumping up and down as I held my own one-year-old child in my arms, releasing the word "NO" from my vocal cords.

The only relief I had that came out of this situation was that I never saw the face of that child. I thank God for what I was spared in the days, weeks, months, and years to come. I did not have the image of that child's face in my mind's eye to replay over and over again. That alone was huge for me.

I later learned that the little boy's dad had

gone into a mechanic's shop while he and his mom sat in their car across the highway from the place. Apparently, the little boy just wanted to be with his dad. So he decided to quietly slip out of the back door of their car, the one not facing the highway. Then, however, he proceeded to make a mad dash to cross the road and join his dad.

Back in the day when this happened, there were no laws concerning restraining children in car seats. That's just how it was back then.

I just so happened to be at that very location at that very moment in time when this little boy decided to make his mad dash across the highway. He hit the side of my van, slid in between the front and back tires, and landed against the back axle. What are the odds for such a thing?

Immediately the sirens were heard, and he was taken to the hospital, while I was taking my first ride ever in a police car. I was twenty-two years old at the time of the accident and never had I ever been involved with any law or court by any means.

I was being taken in because it was mandatory. Anyone involved in this type of accident must submit a blood sample and undergo a Breathalyzer test. This was to rule out me being under the influence of any drugs or alcohol.

Of course, it all came back negative, but still, I will always remember that police car ride, for it was then, at that very moment, I was told that the child had died while on his way to the hospital. When I heard those words, I literally felt my blood run cold throughout my body. A precious little three-year-old child's life had ended that day, and I was attached to that dreadful situation.

What I have learned throughout the years is that whatever the enemy means for harm God will turn around for our good—somehow. It may not seem at the current moment that it is possible, but in due time, it will be revealed.

Just days before that accident I had been invited to a prayer meeting being held a few days later. Would you call this a coincidence? No, I would have to sum this up as being a divine appointment.

The accident and the prayer meeting both occurred two weeks before Christmas. With that in mind, I found myself attending that prayer meeting. At this point in time, my guard was down. It had been just two days since the accident, and I didn't think twice about going. Why would I *not* go? At the conclusion of that prayer meeting, I had my very first unaware encounter with the courts of Heaven.

The one thing I remembered about that night is that I was asked if I wanted to "get saved," and if I wanted to receive Holy Spirit. I was just like many others. Huh? Get saved? Get filled with Holy Spirit? It was oblivious to what that all really meant, but it sounded good. Yes, I wanted to get saved. From what, I wasn't sure. But, "Yes, let's do this," and, "yes, I'll take Holy Spirit as well."

I came to realize, as the years went by, that many times people come to know Jesus through some form of tragedy. It may not look like my tragedy, but nevertheless it is a form of tragedy that is devastating to them. In those times, the guard walls come down, and they find themselves going with the flow.

God, who is loving, wastes nothing from our lives. He uses it all, even the tragedies. When a tragedy brings a person to Him, He can use it for good.

What I see happening many times is this: when a person becomes vulnerable, they accept Jesus for the need of help or for relief from something, for that moment in time, even though they don't understand why they need to be saved. They eventually go through life for months, even years, not knowing why they needed it, why it was so important. They are saved, and you see fruit coming from their lives. But, if you asked them, they could not tell you what led them to need salvation. I will explain that point a little later.

Coming back to the prayer meeting, I was led in what is called the sinner's prayer. I asked God to forgive me of my sins and to wash me clean. I asked Jesus to be my personal Lord and Savior right then and there. I wish I could tell you that I had goose bumps, that I got slain on the floor, or that I had a wonderful, glorious experience in the things of God in that moment. But, no, there was nothing. I took it by faith. I learned that term as I grew in the things of God.

I have much to be thankful for. God has been so gracious to me. He showed up immediately in the days following my decision to the point that my life was visibly different and Holy Spirit was moving in it, leading me and guiding me each day.

This now leads me to the present, when He was giving me insight into my first encounter with the courts of Heaven.

My very first unaware encounter that connected with the courts of Heaven looked like this:

As I stated before, spiritual courts are seen in the principles of the Word of God. There are many scriptures that we can draw from to present a case. My first case brought me before God, who presides as Judge over all. I entered what would be considered, the Blood Court, where the Courts of Reconciliation and Redemption would be viewed. Here are a few scriptures pertaining to this court. Also, I gave a scriptural base from Luke 18:1-8 for this court in an earlier chapter that you can go back to and reference.

The Heavenly Court:

> *No, you have come to Mount Zion, to the city of the living God, the heavenly Jerusalem, and to countless thousands of angels in a joyful gathering. You have come to the assembly of God's firstborn children,*

*whose names are written in heaven.
You have come to God himself, who
is the judge over all things. You have
come to the spirits of the righteous
ones in heaven who have now been
made perfect. You have come to Jesus,
the one who mediates the new covenant between God and people, and
to the sprinkled blood, which speak of
forgiveness instead of crying out for
vengeance like the blood of Abel.*
                    Hebrews 12:22-24, NLT

The Court of Reconciliation:

*And through [the intervention of] the
Son to <u>reconcile</u> all things to Himself,
making peace [with believers] <u>through
the blood</u> of His cross; through Him, [I
say,] whether things on earth or things
in heaven.*   Colossians 1:20, AMP
                    (Emphasis Mine)

*In fact, the law requires that nearly
everything be cleansed with the blood,*

and without the shedding of <u>blood</u> there is no forgiveness. Hebrews 9:22
(Emphasis Mine)

Since we have been <u>justified by blood</u>, how much more shall we saved from God's wrath through him! For if, while we were God's enemies, we were <u>reconciled</u> to him through the death of his Son, how much more, <u>having been reconciled</u>, shall we be saved through his life! Romans 5:9-10 (Emphasis Mine)

The Court of Redemption:

In him we have <u>redemption</u> through his <u>blood</u>, the <u>forgiveness</u> of sins, in accordance with the riches of God's grace. Ephesians 1:7
(Emphasis Mine)

In whom we have <u>redemption</u> through his <u>blood</u>, even the <u>forgiveness</u> of sins. Colossians 1:14, KJV
(Emphasis Mine)

Forasmuch as ye know that ye were not <u>redeemed</u> with corruptible things, as silver and gold, from your vain conversation received by tradition from your fathers; but with the precious <u>blood</u> of Christ, as of a lamb without blemish and without spot.   1 Peter 1:18-19, KJV
(Emphasis Mine)

When I prayed the sinner's prayer that night, in all reality, it seemed as if nothing had taken place. It seemed as if I went back home the same as before. But something great and glorious *had* happened. I mentioned earlier not to be afraid to come into the courts of Heaven because great things do happen there, and this is one of them.

If I would have been allowed to see into the spiritual realm that night, I would not have walked away thinking that nothing had come of it all. If my spiritual eyes and ears had been opened, I could have seen myself coming into the realm of the courts of Heaven by faith where God, the Righteous Judge, presides over all. He would have been sitting high upon the bench of the court, which is also known as His throne. I would have seen myself entering this court by the blood of Jesus, to petition the court for the forgiveness of my sin, so that I could be pardoned from it and, thus, be aligned back into unity with God, who was originally my Father but whom I had lost contact with.

Looking toward to one side of the court, I would have witnessed the enemy, Satan, raising his voice in accusation, claiming his rights to me before God. Within a second, my eyes would have taken hold of Jesus, who was standing up to defend me as my Attorney, my Lawyer. I would have heard Him pleading on my behalf before the Righteous Judge, based on the finished work of the Lord Jesus Christ Himself, that God would grant me a verdict of not guilty, that the shedding of His blood would cleanse me and buy me back from Satan. Based on that, I would have witnessed the Righteous Judge raising His gavel and proclaiming, "I hereby order the courts that the said petitioner, Emelda, is granted a not guilty verdict. She has been released from the power of Satan and is now a child of the Most High God. She has been purchased by the blood of the Lamb, the Lord Jesus Christ Himself, and her name is now written in the Book of Life. Glory!

I didn't realize the magnitude of the sinner's prayer that night because I wasn't able to see it in this way. In all reality, based on the Word of God, this is exactly what took place.

Let me state a fact that is crucial: There is a difference between coming before an earthly court and coming before a heavenly court. When we stand before an earthly court, we are always innocent until proven guilty. When we stand before the heavenly court for salvation, we are always guilty. Then, we are made innocent through Christ.

God is totally awesome. Little did I know that what the enemy meant for harm toward me on that dreadful day of my accident would set in motion a journey, and many years later, Holy Spirit would say to me,

"Let me take you back on your journey of operating in the courts of heaven, times when you walked in its principles, its concepts, which led you to what are called 'unaware encounters.'"

I mentioned earlier that heavenly and earthly courts mirror one another. This is one of those times when we can see just that. God forgiving me brought me into another court that is seen in the Scriptures. It brought me into the Court of Adoption.

The legal process people go through when wanting to adopt a child is quite costly. It is far from being free. A crazy amount of money is involved. Those who want to be parents have counted the cost and their love for a child overrides that cost.

We can also see that the price was quite costly in the Court of Adoption in Heaven as well. Although we ourselves do not put up any monies to obtain our adoption, it is far from being free. The love of the Father overrode the cost of giving His Son for us. The adoption cost was paid by the blood of Jesus Himself. It produced the legal citizenship we come to know as becoming a child of God, an adoptee. Entering the Court of Redemption led us straight into the Court of Adoption. The two courts work hand in hand.

Adoption scriptures for the courts:

But when the set time had fully come, God sent his Son, born of a woman, born under the law, to redeem those under the law, that we might receive adoption to sonship. Galatians 4:4-5

God decided in advance to adopt us into his own family by bringing us to himself through Jesus Christ. This is what he wanted to do, and it gave him great pleasure. Ephesians 1:5, NLT

For ye have not received the spirit of bondage again to fear, but ye have received the Spirit of adoption, whereby we cry, Abba, Father.

Romans 8:15, KJV

CHAPTER 4

My Second Unaware Encounter
(SUMMONED TO COURT, RESCUE ME)

Within the Christian community, I was considered a "baby Christian." In time, I would grow in the things of God. Three or four months after the tragic accident, I was outside one day mowing my lawn. I didn't realize that my house phone had been ringing. It was not until I had finished cutting the grass that my ear caught the ringing, and I ran inside to answer.

Just in passing, this was long before cellphones. Today they seem to be a part of our bodies.

I said, "Hello."

Then I heard a woman's voice sigh and say, "Finally." As it turned out, this was not a tragic finally but a sweet relief finally. It was a lady by the name of Loretta Landry I had met at a prayer meeting, but not the same prayer meeting where I had given my life to Jesus. This one was different.

Loretta continued, "I felt the Lord wanted me to call and give you a scripture, but you were not answering." She said she had been calling for some time and had finally told the Lord, "Lord, I'm giving it one more try. If Emelda doesn't answer her phone, I'm not calling again. I will count it as just me overthinking and feeling that I needed to give her a scripture."

Glory to God, I *did* answer the call, and she proceeded to tell me the scripture she had received from the Lord for me. It was this:

No weapon formed against thee shall prosper; and every tongue that shall rise against thee in judgement thou shalt condemn. This is heritage of the servants of the LORD, and their righteousness is of me, saith the LORD.

Isaiah 54:17, KJV

In all honesty, I had absolutely no clue what she had just said to me. None! Absolutely none! But I thanked her for being obedient and giving me the message from God.

Then the day came, about two weeks later, when I was home alone and was suddenly being served a subpoena—of all things. Why in the world would I be getting a subpena? I knew I was not in trouble with the law.

Without skipping a beat, the deliverer pronounced, "You are being sued for an accident that you were a part of." Right then and there I remembered. Oh, how I remembered, and fear gripped my heart. I started shaking uncontrollably. It seemed to come from the inside out.

Then, instantaneously, something happened. There was a shifting. It happened immediately, quickly. From deep within me, words came bursting forth. It was the scripture given to me:

No weapon formed against thee shall prosper; and every tongue that

SHALL RISE AGAINST THEE IN JUDGEMENT THOU SHALT CONDEMN. THIS IS HERITAGE OF THE SERVANTS OF THE LORD, AND THEIR RIGHTEOUSNESS IS OF ME, SAITH THE LORD.

Wow! In the twinkling of an eye, a peace came over me. For some reason, that word brought me peace in that situation, and I was no longer afraid. It was just like, poof, all that fear was gone, and the shaking subsided.

I knew by then that the accident had been deemed a "no fault" situation, and I had not been given a ticket because of that. Naturally speaking, that should have given me peace. But that is not where the peace came from. It came from the promise of Isaiah 54:17 that had come alive in me.

When I thought about it, I realized that Holy Spirit had known I was going to be served with a legal action that would summon me to court, and He had prepared me with that scripture days in advance. He knew I was going to need it. Again, I was just a baby Christian, and yet He was doing this for me.

The accuser may have served me here on earth with his subpoena, but my Daddy was already at work on my behalf days before. Daddy God had already notified me, serving me papers straight from the courts of Heaven to let me know that He was going to defend me.

This is one of those God encounter moments when He came and encountered me from His courts, an encounter that has left a great mark on my life. God showed Himself strong on my behalf although in those moments I could not yet see the complete fullness of it.

Let me tell you how great my Daddy is. He kept me from going to court. Sure enough, to this very day, it has been forty-three years that I have never put a single foot into a courtroom concerning this matter. From early on, He also removed the sting of that accident from me. I have the comfort, knowing from Scriptures, that the child is alive and well in Heaven.

When I speak of this accident, it is like I am telling a foreign story, a story that I was never a part of. Daddy has taken care of whatever the enemy could have used in this situation to destroy me. God is so good!

My Second Unaware Encounter

My second unaware encounter that connected me with the courts of Heaven was this:

The Scriptures warn us that we have an accuser, an adversary who wants to build cases of accusations against us. He wants to bring us before the court of God to defile us.

My first encounter brought me to a place of right standing with my Daddy God, where the precious blood of Jesus, my Savior, took care of that in the courts of Redemption and Reconciliation. My second encounter also took place in the Courts of Redemption, where God is Judge as well. I mentioned earlier from scripture that we approach God as Judge also when such cases are being formed against us. It is in this court that I needed Jesus to be my Advocate, to preside over an accusation case pending against me.

Now let's take a closer look at this case.

Who will bring any charge against those whom God has chosen? God is the one who justifies.   Romans 8:33

The adversary, the accuser, was trying to build a case against me in the earthly courts due to the accident. He was saying I was at fault and I needed to pay up to make things right. But Jesus, the Lord Himself, took care of my case in the heavenly courts. He became my Advocate, interceded on my behalf, and pleaded my case for me.

I was told that I needed to stand on the Word that God had given me, and I was told to speak this aloud. Being a newborn baby Christian, I didn't yet know all the principles of the Word of God and how to operate in them. All I had was that word the sister had given me, just one scripture to hold onto, one scripture to speak out and believe God for. That word given stood as proxy for me, and Jesus, my Advocate, pleaded my case based on that word before the heavenly Judge, asking that He would silence the accuser on my behalf concerning this matter.

God, who is a righteous Judge, rendered a verdict on my behalf, ruling in my favor that I would be released from that lawsuit.

Supernaturally, a verdict was rendered in my favor, and it was over.

> *Therefore he [Jesus] is able to <u>save</u> completely those who come to God through him, because he always lives to <u>intercede</u> for them.*   Hebrews 7:25
>   (Emphasis Mine)

I know this promise concerns salvation, but the word *save* is translated from the Greek word *sozo*, which means "to save, heal, preserve, rescue, restore, and recover." I believe there is no limit to God when He wants to save and rescue us in all situations.

I needed saving. I needed someone to rescue me from this incident. As far as I know, that case has never made it to court. My scripture, Isaiah 54:17, said that no weapon formed against me would prosper. None! And nothing ever did. This was a supernatural encounter in which Jesus pled my case. Glory to God, for His mercy never fails.

As a side note concerning the fact that there is a real adversary, an accuser who wants to accuse you before God, here are a few promises to familiarize yourself with:

> *When you go with your <u>adversary</u> to the <u>magistrate</u>, make every effort along the way to settle with him, lest he drag you to the judge, the judge deliver you to the officer, and the officer throw you into prison.* Luke 12:58, NKJV
> (Emphasis Mine)

This scripture is saying that there are times we do need to handle our business before we get dragged into court. If we know we're at fault, we must admit it, repent of it, and move on.

> *On another day the angels came to present themselves before the LORD, and Satan also came with them to present himself before him. And the LORD said to Satan, "Where have you come from?" Satan answered the Lord, "From roaming throughout the earth, going back and forth on it."*

Then ther Lord *said to Satan, "Have you considered my servant Job? There is no one on earth like him; he is blameless and upright, a man who fears God and shuns evil. And he still maintains his integrity, though you incited me against him to ruin him without any reason."*

"Skin for skin!" Satan replied. "A man will give all that he has for his own life. But now stretch out your hand and strike his flesh and bones, and he will surely curse you to your face."

The Lord *said to Satan, "Very well, then, he is in your hands; but you must spare his life."*   Job 2:1-6

And I heard a loud voice saying in heaven, Now is come salvation, and strength, and the kingdom of our God, and the power of his Christ: for the accuser *of our brethren is cast down, which* accused *them before our God day and night.*   Revelation 12:10, KJV
(Emphasis Mine)

CHAPTER 5

My Third Unaware Encounter
(SUMMONED TO COURT ONCE AGAIN)

I have read that there is a court in Heaven where the angels are worshipping the Lord God, who is the King of Kings and Lord of Lords, night and day. They are always before the face of God. I am not implying that I have been to Heaven and seen the face of God in that court. How awesome that would be! But I do have an experience that I hold very dear within my heart.

This encounter I more or less kept to myself until now. I am sure that others have experienced what I did. I am nobody special for this to have happen to, and yet it did.

One night, I put my children to bed and crawled into my own bed for the night. As I lay there, quieting down from the day, I felt a nudge. It was not that someone touched me; it was something I felt inside, a sensing that I should get up and pray. It was not as if I had not prayed that day; I had. Apparently, I was a little tired, and this made me a little insensitive to the nudge, so I called it a night.

The next day dawned and then came the night, and once again, as I lay in my bed, I felt that nudge within, that feeling that I needed to arise, go into my living room, and pray. I remember it as if it just happened.

This time I obeyed. I got up, made my way into the living room, and got down on my knees in that kind of sitting position in which you are bent over facing the floor. My sofa was only a few feet in front of me.

The precious thing about that night was that I didn't have to do anything to try to get my prayer going. The minute I cupped my face with my hands, I began praying, and my prayer led to weeping. There was a cry coming from way down deep inside of me.

I knew it was a supernatural encounter taking place. That was for sure, but I really cannot say that I remember my surroundings. I guess I took it for granted that I was still in my living room. What I *do* know is that I was still bent over facing down, my face covered by my hands and my eyes shut.

Then, suddenly, it was as if I was seeing straight ahead of me. I wasn't looking down anymore, even though I was still bent over facing down. In time, I came to realize that these were my spiritual eyes looking ahead of me, and they were beholding a Person sitting on my sofa. In that moment, I was not focused on whether or not it was actually my sofa. It was the aftereffects of the encounter that caused such wondering, as I was wanting to make sense of it all.

If it sounds like I had lost a marble or two, I have to agree, but this was for real. This really took place. What my eyes were beholding was the Lord Jesus Christ, the King of Kings and Lord of Lords sitting on what I assumed was my sofa. I assumed this because that was what was in front of me when I had first knelt to pray. I never saw His face, although I did see the rest of

Him sitting there. He was wearing a bright white robe. The atmosphere was different, of course. It was quite overwhelming.

During that encounter, a great peace came over me. It was a peace like I had never experienced before, and that peace was very tangible. I must emphasize just how authentic it really was. There was a substance around me and in me. I could lay hold of it ... if you can understand what I'm saying.

That supernatural peace remained on me for three full days and nights. After the third day, I knew it had lifted. It was not that I didn't still have peace, but that tangible presence was no longer there.

It's a funny thing that when one has an encounter, especially if it happened while you were still a baby Christian, you may just want to jump into that religious mode again. What I'm saying is this: in that moment, being facetious, I kind of looked at the sofa as maybe a little sacred, maybe a little holy. Why? Because I assumed that the encounter Jesus and I had shared was while He was sitting on that sofa.

I didn't go overboard with it. It was only a fleeting thought. I eventually gave the sofa away, but I forever have treasured in my heart what happened that night.

Many years later, after laptops became popular, I came across a picture and I became undone. I know it's hard for young people to fathom a time when that technology was not available, but I'm from an older generation.

Coming back to the picture. It was exactly how I saw Jesus sitting in His glory on my sofa, except that in this picture, He was sitting on His throne. Once again, you could not see His face, but He was arrayed in His robe of white.

This was another of those God encounter moments that came straight from Heaven. This time, He came to encounter me once again from His courts. He was pursuing me. My thoughts for the day were done, and I was preparing for sleep, but God's thoughts were not my thoughts. His thoughts were higher than mine. He was preparing to have a date with me that night.

Who would have ever thought that Jesus would want to do such a thing, but He did, and this became another treasured encounter I had with Him, leaving another mark of His presence upon my life.

My Third Unaware Encounter

My third unaware encounter that connected with the courts of Heaven was this:

This encounter began with a royal invitation given by the King of Kings from the courts of Heaven. I was being gently summoned by God, my Father. In this encounter, He presented Himself to me as He is—Jesus, King of Kings and Prince of Peace. The Father knows us all too well that we, as mortals, relate to Jesus a little more since He became as one of us.

This encounter did not take place in an open court for all to view. I was summoned to His inner chamber, which is private, where only I had eyes to see. It was a visitation that He desired and hoped that I would accept.

As noted, I was invited twice before I accepted this invitation. How many times has God summoned us to come before Him and we have declined His invitation? How many blessings have we fortified? Only He knows. May we all be a little more sensitive to the gentle nudges within.

My suggestion to you is that when you feel a nudge, when you feel that unction to go pray, go! You may never know what heavenly encounter is in store and what God wants to bestow on you.

Those nudges I felt were not just nudges, as I had assumed. No, they were the gentle summoning's of my King for time spent in His inner chamber. It revealed my personal relationship with Him, or should I say, His personal relationship with me. That's more like it. Maybe we need to grasp the fact that He really longs to be with us. To meditate on that alone is huge.

As I reflect on this encounter, I cannot help but think of Queen Esther. One night the King summoned her, and she obtained favor in his sight. I, too, in the presence of my King, was given the favor of His peace that passes all understanding.

How I thank God that I did not listen to my flesh that night, that I did not roll over and go to sleep as I had done the night before. I would have missed what He wanted to impart to me. I cannot tell you that this has ever happened again. It has not. I don't know if He will ever choose to reveal Himself to me again in this way. I'm just grateful that He did, and I will never forget it.

I love the Word of God and want to take space here to share some scriptures revealing that Jesus and the Father are one, along with scriptures that say we can obtain favor and receive peace from Him.

> *Philip said, "Lord, show us the Father and that will be enough for us."*
> *Jesus answered: "Don't you know me Philip, even after I have been among you such a long time? Anyone who has seen me has seen the Father. How can you say, 'Show us the Father'? Don't you believe that I am in the Father, and that the Father is in me? The words I say to you I do not speak of my own authority. Rather, it is the Father, living in me, who is doing his work."* John 14:8-10

> *I and the Father are one.* John 10:30

101

On that day you will realize that I am in my Father, and you are in me, and I am in you. John 14:20

May the LORD show you his favor and give you his peace.
Numbers 6:26, NLT

This spiritual court also mirrors our earthly courts. In our earthly courts, there is a court within a court. Legal affairs are held in the public courts. This is where the jury, the witnesses, and the public are allowed to view the proceedings.

Then there are times, when conditions are just right, that a court hearing has the potential to lead to a private hearing. This is called "in chambers," and these chambers are often located on the upper floors of the courthouse, away from the public courtrooms. Such a chamber is closed to the public and to the media, and no one is allowed to observe what is going on there. This chamber is only for the participants.

This court, this chamber, reflects the inner chamber of the Holy of Holies, where God's presence abides. The heavenly pattern of the Tabernacle that was given to Moses consisted of three courts. There was the Outer Court, the Holy Court, and the Holy of Holies, which was the inner court or the innermost chamber.

Here, too, we see there are courts within a court. The inner court, which was the Holy of Holies, was located away from the other courts. This court, this inner chamber, was closed off to the public. Only the High Priest was allowed to enter the Holy of Holies, the most inner chamber.

According to the Scriptures, as one who has been cleansed by the blood of Jesus, we too, are known as special people:

But you are a chosen people, a royal priesthood, a holy nation, God's special possession, that you may declare the praises of him who called you out of darkness into his wonderful light. 1 Peter 2:9

This is what enabled Jesus, my King, to invite me into His holy chamber, His court, and there I was able to experience such a glorious encounter with Him.

CHAPTER 6

My Fourth Unaware Encounter
(STANDING IN PROXY)

After I was born again, I began attending a church that believed in intercessory prayer. Once a week we met to pray, and these meetings were powerful. We saw many results come forth from them. Holy Spirit reminded me of one specific night.

That night seemed like any other. I had begun praying in English, which we call "praying in the natural," but eventually I slipped into my heavenly language (which I had received when I was filled with Holy Spirit). Before long, once again I found myself experiencing that realm of the suddenlies.

Now my praying shifted and took off, and when it did, I took off too. In this realm, it was as though I had taken on the burden, the struggle, the intensity of what someone else was enduring at the time. As I proceeded to pray, I lost the awareness of everyone around me. I had entered a realm which I am still learning about today. It is where intercessory prayer is attached to operating in the courts of Heaven.

Until then, intercessory prayer had been on a different level. I knew I was making a difference in the spirit realm. I was standing in the gap for someone. It was rather like fighting in the atmosphere. At the time, I had no concept that it was somehow tied to the courts of Heaven, for I had never envisioned it that way.

Coming back to that night when that sudden shift took place, I took on whatever that person was going through. I can recall vividly the agony, the stronghold that was on that person. I became one with it, and my prayer was unrelenting. All I could do was groan. These groanings were out of this world intense, deep, agonizing groans. I was so caught up in the situation of that person.

I had entered the warfare that took place concerning this prayer suddenly, and it also ended suddenly.

I am reminded of Roman 8:26-27 (NKJV):

Likewise the Spirit also helps in our weaknesses. For we do not know what we should pray for as we ought, but the Spirit Himself makes intercession for us with groanings which cannot be uttered. Now He who searches the hearts knows what the mind of the Spirit is, because He makes intercession for the saints according to the will of God.

Although I said I entered this prayer suddenly and that it ended suddenly, I'm not saying that my prayer was short. No, I was laboring for some time in the Spirit. Let me tell you how it ended. This is the best part of all.

Just before the struggle broke, I heard the voice of God audibly. His voice was so clear. It brings tears to my eyes even more as I'm writing this. When He spoke, He spoke with great authority. Suddenly, I heard Him say, "IT'S OVER! IT'S FINISHED! SHE'S DELIVERED!" And just like that all the agony and the heaviness lifted from me, and I was back in my natural frame of mind. It was phenomenal how in a millisecond the struggle and the deliverance converged.

I was overwhelmed by this encounter. It was one of my first times of truly standing in the gap for someone, with this kind of result manifesting, with the manifestation of hearing the voice of God and knowing that my prayer had accomplished what needed to be done. That was all great and glorious, but I didn't know who I was praying for specifically that night.

Two days later, however, it was revealed. The Lord had me standing in the gap for someone in my own bloodline, someone very dear to me, someone who came to know the Lord but, for whatever reason, got caught up in a bad situation.

What was brought to my attention about that night was this: at that very moment, my loved one and their friend decided to take some form of drug, supposing it was a mixture of this and that. Apparently, they failed to get the high they thought they would. Instead, the experience turned out horribly bad. I was told their bodies were going into paralysis, along with other ill effects. I'm not sure how the emergency call got made, but it did. The friend was taken to the hospital to get immediate help. On the other hand, the one I was interceding for received deliverance by the mighty hand of God.

As I am writing this, I sense Holy Spirit is saying, "Surely, they both could have been delivered that same night through prayer." He said, "It is not that the friend was not loved like the other by the Father. The friend's deliverance came from the hands of a physician, whereas your loved one got delivered by the hand of God."

My fourth unaware encounter with the courts of Heaven was this:

This realm, that of God as Friend, is revealed in the courts of Heaven. I mentioned in an earlier chapter that this is seen in Luke 11:5-8, where a man went to a friend to help another friend because he himself didn't have the means to do it. We can see throughout the Scriptures the principle of this court process in action as people were used by God.

> *For the eyes of the LORD run to and fro throughout the whole earth, to shew himself strong in the behalf of them whose heart is perfect toward him.*
>
> 2 Chronicles 16:9, KJV

> *And I sought for a man among them who should build up the wall and stand in the breach before me for the land, that I should not destroy it, but I found none.* Ezekiel 22:30, ESV

I [Jesus] no longer call you servants, because a servant does not know his master's business. Instead, I have called you friends, for everything that I learned from my Father I have made known to you.   John 15:15

And the scripture was fulfilled which says, "Abraham believed God, and it was accounted to him for righteousness." And he was called the friend of God.
                    James 2:23, KJV

Abraham was able to interceded on behalf of his family who lived in Sodom. Because he was a friend of God, the Lord did not hide from him His thoughts of destroying the city (see Genesis 18).

In these few scriptures, we can see the heart of God. He wants to reveal His thoughts to us so that we can pray and make intercession on behalf of others. What an honor it is to be considered a friend of God! We, too, have a Friend who sticks closer than a brother. He is Jesus who ever lives to make intercession for us in the courts of Heaven, as seen in Hebrews 7:25:

Therefore he is able to save completely those who come to God through him, because he always lives to intercede for them.

What Holy Spirit revealed on that night of intercessory prayer was this: God considered me His friend with a situation where He, as Friend, wanted to show Himself strong. It came by way of prayer. He used me to stand in the gap for a loved one, to stand before His court on their behalf, so they could be set free.

I did not work alone in this prayer. As is stated in Romans 8:26-27, I also had the help of Holy Spirit alongside me praying. I was only the vessel He used to stand as proxy for my loved one before the throne of grace in the courts of Heaven.

In the *Merriam-Webster Dictionary*, the meaning of the word *proxy* is "a person who is given the power or authority to do something for someone else." Standing in proxy is standing in the gap, and that's exactly what took place that night.

CHAPTER 7

My Fifth Unaware Encounter
(A JUST JUDGE)

If you are anything like me, at one time or another I am sure you have handed out Christian tracts to others. There is a particular one that I am very fond of. It is called "ONE WAY." This is my absolute favorite tool. This tract is something I often use to teach from. In the early chapters, I said there was a special tool that I liked. This was it.

You may wonder why. What's the big deal with this tract? The reason I have always been drawn to it is due to its simplicity. It delivers the salvation message without question, but in pictorial form. It is all laid out there. You may have figured out by now that I love using visuals to teach.

Within the illustrations of this tract, there are legal and binding aspects of the

Kingdom taking place. As I turned each page of this tract, I saw what my heart and my mind already perceived. They revealed that God was and is a just God and that He handles salvation in a legal manner.

I knew this legal matter could not be overlooked. However, when we become born again, we are normally drawn to God because of His great love toward us. That is the view we are beholding. Yet, there is a side in the salvation message that may go unnoticed for a while. You may say, "I know God is a just God." I believed that too, but I failed to see the full picture or meaning of it in its entirety. In my earlier walk with the Lord, I didn't perceive salvation teachings that pointed to the concept of any court. When teaching on salvation, I never veered in that direction as I do now. All I knew was that I was very adamant about a legal issue, and with the using of this tool, I was able to express what my heart and mind already knew.

From that point on, I felt Holy Spirit leading me to use this tool in children's ministry.

Seeing the simplicity in those illustrations, I took the time to select several of them and greatly enlarged the ones I had chosen. I was sure they would catch the children's attention. I laminated them and eventually I stretched them across the wall in the children's church classroom. This was my Spirit-given tool, and I was going to use it.

I incorporated time in my classes to review the story of Adam and Eve. Eventually the children were able to tell me what really took place in Eden. These were seeds sown in their hearts that laid a foundation for the fact that God has a legal order that He stands by. It was something Holy Spirit would be able to build on in the days, weeks, months, and years to come, to further the understanding of those children on this subject. Looking back, this was their first introduction to the courts of Heaven, although I myself didn't even realize it at the time.

The use of this tool was not limited to the classroom. For our Good Friday Celebrations, we would have family and some of our friends over. My class was big that day. Our Good Fridays were not just a day for eating boiled crawfish and crabs as we do in the Deep South. Although that is a highlight of our day, and we did eat, I planned a whole day with games and prizes reflecting Jesus.

We had the typical egg hunt, and then everyone gathered afterward to hear the Easter story. In numbered sequence, the children handed me the resurrection eggs they had picked up during their hunt. Each egg held a clue to what took place on Good Friday that eventually led to the resurrection of Jesus.

Other plastic eggs contained tokens the children were able to redeem for prizes. This was accomplished by them throwing a dart into red balloons that were arranged in the shape of a cross. We also had a time for popcorn and a movie that was centered on what Jesus did for us that day, and adults were included.

This became a ritual on Good Friday. I would pull out my extra set of that long, stretched-out banner of illustrations. As we gathered outside, the banner would get pinned to the wall of the house. At some point, everyone would gather on the grounds, and I would go over the salvation message.

I interacted with my grandchildren as well as with the adults. They were not exempt from the message of this little tract.

In an earlier chapter, I mentioned that many times when one becomes vulnerable, they accept Jesus for the need of help or relief of something, even if, in that moment, they don't understand why they need to be saved. This is not limited to people who have experienced tragedy. I see this in many new believers. I guess that is why I am adamant about this tract. This truth is there for all to see. It starts and finishes with God who is righteous and who is a just Judge, who handles the affairs of our lives in a legal manner.

The pamphlet begins with God walking in the garden, communing with Adam and Eve, just the way it was supposed to be. In the next illustration, God is standing with one hand pointing to the tree. With the other hand, His palm is facing toward the couple with the word NO! That speaks for itself.

The story continues with Adam and Eve standing in front of the tree by themselves, just gazing upon it. But, as we all know, there is the picture of Eve reaching for the fruit, and then she eats it. This sequence is followed by Adam.

The next scene is a dreadful picture. There is no longer a beautiful garden that God created. From the tree, it is now raining down gloomy streams of darkness. In the middle of the tree there is a skull with two bones marking an X through it. The word SIN is also raining down. It is the most awful picture you could ever want to see.

Then we come upon Adam and Eve as they were examining themselves. Their clothing, their skin and their surroundings were no longer the same. Before they had been clean and vibrant. Now they are standing in utter filth. They now have some sort of black "stuff" on their skin, and they are giving off an odor. You can see vapors coming from their bodies.

The sad part about all this comes in the next illustration. In this one, they are standing before God. He is still in all of His glory, but they are standing there before Him in their filth, with their heads hanging down, knowing they have done wrong.

Then God has His arm extended, just as He did toward the tree, but this time, it is meant for them. His palms are extended to them, letting them know they can no longer come near Him. They can no longer be in His presence. Wow! What a game changer.

And it gets worse! In the next illustration, God Almighty is building a wall between them. It is not that *He* actually built the wall. It was actually the sin of disobedience that built it. That is what caused the separation.

Later, you can see Adam and Eve in the river, trying to wash off the filth from their bodies. It was the stain of sin that came upon them from disobeying God. Although they try to wash it off, they cannot remove it.

In the next few scenes, we see that they have children. You would think that these children would not have to carry the sin of their parents, but they do. The children are covered in the same filth of sin.

Wherefore, as by one man sin entered into the world, and death by sin; and so death passed upon all men, for that all have sinned. Romans 5:12, KJV

It was for this reason alone that God needed to send Jesus back to earth to come redeem us, to buy us back from Satan. I know that is a hard saying, but it is the truth.

In whom the god of this world hath blinded the minds of them which believe not, lest the light of the glorious gospel of Christ, who is the image of God, should shine unto them.
2 Corinthians 4:4, KJV

God had given Adam all authority in the earth, and the earth was for him to keep and watch over. But when Adam succumbed to that fruit, he chose to obey Satan's voice instead of God's. In so doing, he handed all his authority over to Satan. The earth became Satan's playground, and he governed it now. So, we all became slaves because of that one sin.

We see within the illustrations, that the earth became populated with multitudes of people. Each one was clothed in the same filth of sin. They were all walking the same road, going in the same direction. Strangely enough, at the end of the road, flames were in view, flames depicting Hell.

But before they come to that dreadful end of the road, there are signs beckoning them to notice a door up ahead. The signs read: "All Are Welcome," "Love Gift Ahead," and "Free Gift." The very last one says, "God's Love Gift Inside."

At the entrance of the door lies a mat that says "All Are Welcome." There is no excuse for anyone to not enter the door and see what God has for them. This is all in full view.

As the people approach this door, it is a very sad scene. Way too many are not even interested in the signs. They are walking on into eternity without God.

Now we see that there are three children who decide to peek. There is a girl and two boys. As they enter the door, they are welcomed by multiple pictures laid out before them. There is a sign under the pictures that says, "One Way" and it has an arrow pointing further into the hall.

The first illustration inside is of Mary holding the Christ Child. The second is of the wise men following the star. The next one is a man being healed by Jesus. Then there is the illustration of our Lord and Savior carrying the cross and being beaten. We know exactly where this leads. It leads to the illustration of Jesus nailed to the cross. The last illustration shows Jesus ascending into Heaven.

As the tract continues in the next scene, Jesus is on the cross upon the hill, and the words "God's Free Love Gift" are displayed under it. The three children who entered the hall and saw all the illustrations are now standing facing and pointing toward Jesus.

Keep in mind that these children are just like Adam and Eve. On their bodies, their clothing, and their surroundings is the stain and stench of sin.

Amazingly enough, two of the children are becoming receptive to the love of Jesus. The other child is expressing that he is not interested at all. The two fall on their knees as they gaze upon Jesus. Their hands are held together as though they are praying. They bend themselves down, facing to the ground, and they give their hearts to Him. In return, streaming from the cross, the blood of Jesus flows and covers them.

In the next illustration, there is the glory shining all around them. Amazingly enough the children are now white and clean.

In the next scene the two children are addressing the boy who did not kneel. They are pointing to the cross. As the boy stands in his filthy rags, he raises his hand and jesters that he wants no part of God's free gift.

Instead, he walks out to join the others who are on the way to destruction.

In the next few illustrations, you see the boy and girl who have given their hearts to Lord. They are pointing upward to where there are stairs before them. These stairs lead right into the presence of God in Heaven. You can sense excitement, rejoicing, and music. Everyone is welcoming them.

The best part of all is Daddy God, Jesus, and Holy Spirit are there with their arms opened wide, eagerly welcoming these little ones. The children make a mad dash to them. Under this illustration is written these powerful words:

For God so loved the world, that he gave his only begotten Son, that whosoever believeth in him should not perish, but have everlasting life.   John 3:16, KJV

My Fifth Unaware Encounter

My fifth unaware encounter with the courts of Heaven was this:

Holy Spirit placed that simple little pamphlet in my hand, and it became my tool to relay the message I was so adamant about. It was the message that God presided as a just Judge and that we had a great need. That need, above all the other needs that we had, was to be bought back from Satan. My message never swerved from these words as I would point toward each illustration.

I spoke on how God, who is the Ruler and Judge over all, stood by His own words. He did not override them for His own convenience or to have His own way. In all honesty, because He is God, He can do whatever He wants. He could have decided it was not necessary to send Jesus to earth to die for us. He could have kicked Satan right off the planet, but He didn't. He could have made all things new and whole again, but He didn't.

Why? For one reason only. God is a just God. He is a just Judge. He is not a corrupt judge. He rules in truth, standing by His own words. This was what I was so adamant about, but I was not viewing this in the way of courtroom activity. That goes to show how we only see in part, and then, in due time, revelation comes. It was something so simple, so overlooked.

My involvement with this realm continued as I went forward in my message about God. "That's right," I concluded, "God gave Adam the authority in the earth. It was for Adam to take care of it. But Adam handed his God-given authority over to Satan on the day he disobeyed God. God had warned him and Eve:

> *You must not eat fruit from the tree that is in the middle of the garden, and you must not touch it, or you will die.*
>
> Genesis 3:3

That was plain and simple. The spirit of man died that day, and he needed to be bought back from Satan from that dreadful moment on."

I did not skip a beat, my words continued: "Adam and Eve were still alive after they took that bite, but their spirit took on a different nature. That is what all that filth was about in the illustrations. Those illustrations depicted the terrible change that had taken place in them. God wanted to rescue, to redeem His children, and He wanted it to be done legally. He lost us in that transaction of Adam's sin. That sin and that sin alone is what separated you and me from God. That prevented us from having a relationship with Him. That is why He sent Jesus who was without sin.

Jesus was not defiled by the sin which got passed down to the rest of us through Adam. No, Jesus' blood was pure and holy. Only Jesus was able to present His blood on the altar in Heaven as a sacrifice so that we could be bought back from Satan legally.

When we ask Jesus to come into our lives as our personal Lord and Savior and to forgive us of sin, He does it at that very moment. You are no longer walking around with that filth on you. You are clean, you are a new creation, you are a now a child of God." That was my message and that pamphlet was my visual tool for all to see that it was reality.

When I would give this message, I didn't yet view it as Jesus being our Attorney or Lawyer or us standing before a court in Heaven. This was something Holy Spirit brought to my attention much later in life. Jesus became our Defense Attorney when we were born again. He stood and pleaded our case against Satan, who is the Prosecuting Attorney. You see, this is having an encounter with the courts. This is court-room activity where judgements are being made on our behalf.

What Holy Spirt revealed was that all along in my spirit I had a firm concept concerning the courts, although it took time for me to realize that God presided over a court or that we had been participating in the courts on so many different levels.

CHAPTER 8

My Sixth Unaware Encounter
(PRAYER ROOM, THRONE ROOM)

I'm sure you're all familiar with the 2015 movie "War Room" that got everyone fired up. Everyone was stripping their closets down to bare walls. All clothing, shoes, purses, and you name it had to find a new home in those houses as the closets were all being turned into prayer rooms.

"War Room" was a very well-made movie, and the anointing was all over it. It was inspiring to see how many people got turned on to the idea of making a war room in their house, their own personal prayer room. Although it was inspiring to see what was taking place for others, this was not a new thing for me.

When we bought our home back in the early 1990s, we were blessed to have two walk-in closets in our master bedroom. They were over-sized, and my husband and I decided that one closet was big enough to share between the two of us. The other closet became mine to do whatever I wanted with. I could have turned it into a sewing and craft room because I enjoy doing that sort of thing. However, that was not how I wanted to make use of it.

I loved the way our home was laid out. Our bedroom was at the very far end of the house, away from the kitchen, the living room, and the kids' rooms. In the coming days, my closet took on a whole new look. Its function was now my prayer room, my study hall, my place to prepare lessons for children's ministry and to do the secretarial work I was doing for the church at the time. It was my place to get alone with Jesus.

That was the best room in the house, to me anyway. My little room was perfect. When I would get in it, I was not distracted by things going on in the rest of the house, and my next encounter happened in that little room.

My Sixth Unaware Encounter

I remember going to my prayer closet to pray one night. There was not anything special going on. It is not like I had that nudging to go pray, like I had experienced several years before. No, I just wanted to pray.

In my prayer closet, my husband had made me an L-shaped desktop. That gave me an adequate amount of space for all my "stuff," and I loved it. Sometimes it does not take much to make a girl happy, and this did the trick. But it also held another special purpose for me.

We all have our preferences when we go to prayer. Some people like to walk, and some like to kneel. You get the picture. As for myself, I like a covering over me. It just gives me a sense of intimacy and closeness to Daddy. My position of preference in my prayer closet, therefore, was for to get on the floor and crawl under that desktop. That just made this time to pray even better. I would get all snuggled up under there, maybe leaning against the wall at times. It was the best. It was my secret place, reserved for Jesus and me.

On the night in question, everything was normal. I made my way under the desktop as my covering, and I began praying. At some point, I stopped and made my way out of the closet. I will tell you right now that I did not sense that anything spectacular had taken place in my prayer room that night. If I said anything to the contrary, I would be lying.

To my surprise, as I made my way out of the room, my eyes fell on a clock on the night stand. I saw my husband lying back in bed, and I thought to myself, "Hmm, he came to bed early tonight."

I looked back at the clock and then asked him if that was the right time. It couldn't have been. But he replied, "Yes, it is."

I found my way to the kitchen and the living room to view the time on the clocks there, and they all had the same time. I suddenly decided that my family must be playing a joke on me. No way had I been in my prayer closet for three hours.

After questioning the kids about the time on the clocks, I called the phone company for the time. I know that makes me sound ancient. Anyway, I quickly realized that my family was not playing a joke on me. Most definitely I had been in there for three hours.

I cannot tell you anything about what took place in those three hours. I wish I could. All I know is that it happened again the next two nights. That was nine hours that I was unable to account for.

Talk about being blown away. When I walked out of that prayer closet and saw that three hours had elapsed and I couldn't account for it, that was wild. I came to the conclusion that I had to count it as a supernatural and heavenly encounter with Daddy. I know for sure that no time is ever wasted with Him.

The question is: was I standing before His throne or somewhere in one of His courts or in His secret place? Whatever that encounter was, I didn't come out of it with fear of any kind. God's presence would not do that to anyone.

My sixth unaware encounter was with my prayer room or the throne room:

Since Holy Spirit included this time frame of my life as part of one of my unaware encounters with the courts of Heaven, I cannot ignore it. Before this, I had not come to any understanding of that encounter. In the years since, I have known it was something of great value. I just didn't have words to describe it. Since I have come to the teachings of the courts, it has opened an avenue for Holy Spirit to minister to me in realms I had walked into but was unaware of it. The same goes for this night. Holy Spirit has breathed life upon it, giving me insight to back up what I wrote earlier. It was simply being in God's presence in His courts.

During the time when this took place, I often sang the chorus *How Lovely Are Your Dwelling Places*. This was taken from Psalm 84. Fast forward to the present time, and I found myself coming back to that song. The words that I kept repeating were:

How lovely are thy <u>dwelling</u> <u>places</u>.
My soul longs for the <u>courts</u> of the Lord.
My heart and my flesh sings for joy to
the living God.
You are my King and my God.

After a time of singing, I was prompted to meditate on the word *courts* and to look at the context of how it was presented in Psalm 84. The word *court* was pertaining to "one longing to be at church, a building, or a temple." But that is not what I was hearing from Holy Spirit. Instead I heard:

"It is not that my soul was longing or crying out to go to a building, but that my soul was crying out for the presence of the Lord, right where I was at that moment."

The song starts off with: "How lovely are Your dwelling places." This brought me back to Psalm 91:1-2 KJV:

He that dwelleth in the secret place of the most High shall abide under the shadow of the Almighty.

The word *dwells* in the *Bible Tool Greek/ Hebrew Definitions Strong's Concordance* #3427: *yashab*, "to sit down, to remain, to settle, to marry: to abide, habitation, make to keep house, marry."

After intense study on Psalm 91 from a few years back and the study of the word *shadow,* it is clear that seeing a shadow means that the real is near. You cannot be under a shadow if the physical object causing the shadow is far from you. I learned that being under the shadow of the Almighty is simply being in the presence of God. I was dwelling somewhere under that shadow, in a secret place where my Daddy was. I was close to Him.

It had seemed that I was going to my prayer closest just to pray, but I had to change the way I thought. We don't just go to pray. Something happens when we pray. Maybe our flesh has that concept, but our spirit is longing for deep intimacy within the courts of God 24/7.

The beauty of God is His manifold wisdom, which, in the Hebrew, comes from the word *rebab*. It means "to become many, numerous, yet streaming from one original source." There are many facets to the words *dwell* and *courts*.

I know for certain that I was not at a church setting seeking God's presence that night. I was in my closet, and something took place there. It was a supernatural encounter. I was somewhere in the Spirit in the courts of the Lord.

Writing about my unaware encounters in His presence has led me to a desire. I so desire to be translated to Heaven. When I go, I want to know I am there. I say, "Why not? Why should this not happen for me? God allows others to partake of and see this realm. I hear testimonies all the time of how God allows people to encounter Heaven like that. They come back with such an impact for His glory, and they are never the same. I desire this, and I have hope that it will take place.

One thing is for sure: I already have one foot in the door. I just want to have both and be able to talk about it when I get to walk in the fullness of Heaven.

> *Delight yourself in the* LORD;
> *And He will give you the desires of your*
> *heart.* Psalm 37:4, NASB

After studying on that specific scripture, I learned that my desires come from God. He has placed them within me. That is why I have been longing for such a thing.

> *Then Jesus told him, "Because you*
> *have seen me, you believed, blessed are*
> *those who have not seen and yet have*
> *believed."* John 20:29

In all reality, I don't need to go to Heaven to believe that God is real. I just want to be there with Him ahead of time. Now I know God wills to whom He wills. But I also know, through scripture, that we have not because we ask not. So, one day do not be surprised when I get the opportunity to tell you of that encounter.

My husband said to me, "Watch what you ask for." I responded, "I don't have to die to go to Heaven. He can just translate me."

When I spoke this to a few of my friends, one of them said, "Why are you asking for that?" My answer was, "I want ... I long for the more."

Once again, I love how Holy Spirit orchestrates people, times, and events in my life. After I had already written about this unexplainable encounter, months later I was watching the Glory Bible Study with Joshua and Janet Mills, and lo and behold, Joshua began to talk about an unusual experience they had in one of their church meetings while traveling. They realized that hours had passed during a specific morning meeting that they were not able to give account for. The realization of this occurred when they caught a glimpse of the time and saw that it was already evening, and people were coming into the church for the night service. Time had elapsed for them as well.

My ears were wide open as he spoke. The way he described this unexplainable time lapse was that: "ETERNITY SWALLOWED UP TIME." How breathtaking! The natural mind cannot comprehend such a thing. On the other hand, the mind of the Spirit comes into full agreement with it. I felt Holy Spirit had His way of confirming my encounter as well. The nine hours that I could not account for were also where eternity had swallowed up time. This was so like Holy Spirit, who loves to reveal things to us in due time.

CHAPTER 9

My Seventh Unaware Encounter
(ORDER IN THE COURT)

Holy Spirit reminded me of another encounter. It happened in December of 2009. It seems as if the month of December keeps popping up. How interesting!

As director of children's ministry in our church, I wanted to have a Christmas performance. In advance, I searched to see what was available, and I came across one that looked peculiar but impressive. It seemed so unoriginal to the Christmas story and not at all the typical play we were used to watching, as our children pranced across the stage, but I was very intrigued by it. I felt that this was THE ONE, and I proceeded to make my purchase.

The name of the play was *The Not-So-Silent Night*. Even the name was a bit strange, and the storyline was very outrageous, totally out of the normal for a Christmas setting.

This play centered around a courtroom. That was very unpredictable for a Christmas play, but you read it right. It was a courtroom setting. How ironic!

The play's opening scene began with a sort of offbeat music. It was loud and bouncy, maybe a bit on the rap side. The man singing it didn't really sing it. He just kind of blurted out the words in a rap tone, "Order in the court! Order in the court! Order in the court."

This was followed by the bailiff pounding his staff on the floor and proclaiming, "All rise! Hear ye, hear ye, hear ye! The district court in and for the County of Bethlehem will now come to order, the honorable Judge Willy Snooze presiding. You may be seated."

I was thrilled beyond measure with this play, to say the least. Can you see how Holy Spirit in some way or another always had courts swirling along my journey. Now He is currently bringing them all together to show me the bigger picture.

Coming back to the play. It started off so offbeat from any other traditional play. At that point, some may have felt like exiting the building. But I can guarantee you, the play was well thought out, and it ended great.

The play was all about the birth of Jesus, and it had it all. There was a judge presiding over his bench, along with the witness stand and several witnesses. Of course, somebody was on trial. We also had the prosecutor sitting behind his desk on one side of the courtroom. On the other side we had the defense attorney ready to defend the defendant.

You may ask, "What happened to the nativity scene?" Oh, we had that too, just not as part of the courtroom setting. The nativity scene was to the far left of the courtroom set.

You may be wondering, "Who was on trial and why did they have to come before this court?" I'm so glad you asked. I was getting to that.

On the far right of the stage, we had the Shepherds Hill. If you are quick to reason things out, you may have figured who was summoned to court. It was those smelly shepherds who saw the star and followed it to Bethlehem. Some of the people of Bethlehem were upset because when the shepherds rode in, they were proclaiming the news very loudly. "To you is born this day in the City of David a Savior, who is the Messiah, the Lord."

After enduring a lengthy trial and reviewing the evidence that the Savior had been born, the shepherds are found worthy of their proclamation and found not guilty for disturbing the peace.

What a great play! I loved it. I loved the fact that it was out of the ordinary and also in a courtroom setting, of all things!

In all honesty, I was able to see what this play was all about. Yet there was a veil upon my eyes that I did not see it in all its entirety. I found myself using the word *entirety* a few times as I wrote. It is so true though. We only see in part. When Holy Spirit decides to show a concept in its entirety, as we may call it, let us not forget there is still more to come. It is only because of the revelation He is showing us at the time that we feel we are seeing the fullness of it.

My seventh unaware encounter with the courts of Heaven was this:

Holy Spirit brought back the play to my remembrance for several reasons. It was to reveal that for some time the Lord had been placing the concepts of the courts of Heaven in my life. Although each encounter looked different from the others, this was an important one.

The other reason was to say, "I know how much you enjoyed working with this play." I surely did. I loved its originality. I loved the courtroom setting. This play was like a gift the Spirit placed in my hand, knowing the joy it would give me. That is what any good father does when he wants to bless his child.

As Holy Spirit showed me that I had had unaware encounters with the courts of Heaven, all the encounters He mentioned were separate and stood alone as far as I was concerned. I never once connected the dots, that all the encounters had some-thing in common. It even came down to me picking out a Christmas play. Who would have imagined! I surely didn't. I was totally unaware of what was taking place.

This is what I was saying earlier. We can operate in the principles and concepts and in the realm of the courts of Heaven on a daily base in the simplest ways and still be totally unaware of it.

Many times, we are blinded and don't see it. So let me suggest to you: ask Holy Spirit to reveal encounters that *you* may have had concerning the courts of Heaven. I am confident that you will be surprised at just how often it takes place.

CHAPTER 10

My Eighth Unaware Encounter
(THE SYMPHONY OF HEAVEN)

I don't know why God chooses to reveal Himself to me in the ways He does. That's His choosing. Who are we to say how He can hand out His blessings?

Despite the fact the following was another encounter that was brought to my attention, I'm a little reluctant to share its content. Its relationship with the courts of Heaven is different than any other encounter.

Taking me by surprise, this encounter started about ten years ago. I was planting flowers, enjoying my day, and minding my own business, when suddenly I was captivated by the sound of creation. This may not sound so intriguing to you, for I know that we have all heard the sounds of chickens clucking or the barking of a dog.

However, the membranes of my ears were suddenly permeated with a virgin sound. As the sound waves entered into the chambers of my ears, they were converted, and the impulses went to my brain, where they were interpreted as sound. This sound came back in word form, and I was in awe of what I was hearing. I was hearing words from creation for the very first time. This was not just a sound, not the sound of a cluck or a bark, but authentic words.

Did you fall off your seat yet? I totally get it. I must agree that it all sounds rather strange. But it has been happening all these years. Yes, I CAN HEAR CREATION PRAISING GOD!

I have had many weird comments or stares because of this. One comment was verbalized in this manner, "Ooooh, okay, Emelda, if you say so, but that is not what I'm hearing." And as this person walked away scratching their heads, they were saying, "Well, you just keep enjoying what you're hearing."

We can clearly see in the Scriptures that all creation does praise God:

My Eighth Unaware Encounter

Praise the LORD.
Praise the LORD from the heavens;
praise him in the heights above.
Praise him, all his angels;
praise him, all his heavenly hosts.
Praise him, sun and moon;
praise him, all you shining stars.
Praise him, you highest heavens
and you waters above the skies.
Let them praise the name of the LORD,
for at his command they were created,
and he established them forever and
ever —
he issued a decree that will never pass
away.
Praise the LORD from the earth,
you great sea creatures and all ocean
depths,
lightning and hail, snow and clouds,
stormy winds that do his bidding,
you mountains and all hills,
fruit trees and all cedars,
wild animals and all cattle,
small creatures and <u>FLYING BIRDS,</u>
kings of the earth and all nations,

you princes and all rulers on earth,
young men and women,
old men and children.
Let them praise the name of the LORD,
for his name alone is exalted;
his splendor is above the earth and the
heavens.
And he has raised up for his people a
horn,
the praise of all his faithful servants,
of Israel, the people close to his heart.
Praise the LORD.   Psalm 148:1-14
                              (Emphasis Mine)

My encounter with Heaven's symphony was none other than the beautiful, euphonious sound of a cardinal praising God, its Creator. Yes, you read that right. And, no, I haven't lost it. I was speechless just as you may be as your read this.

My ears became receptive to the air waves and, in the Spirit, were now the size of an elephant's ears. It was captivating. I stood in amazement as I took it all in. I could not believe what I was perceiving, but it was happening.

Would you like to know the praise song of the majestic red cardinal as Daddy heard it? It was very simple, but it was directed to the Him alone. That's why, I'm sure, it was so captivating.

Cardinal, as I call him, pulsated in this manner, "PRAISE ... PRAISE ... PRAISE YOU!" Every time I hear it, it demands my full attention. I cannot tell you how many times I have grabbed my cellphone to record him. I drop whatever I'm doing and begin a scanning mode if he's not in sight.

I sense the need to find him among the branches. I want to set my sights on him. I want to gaze upon the beauty of his feathers that are of royal red, a reminder of the precious blood of Jesus. No matter where I am when I hear his melody, I immediately come to attention and start scanning the airways to find him.

Over time, Cardinal has come to recognize my voice, and we have a relationship going on. I know he watches for me. As I enter my sunroom, he makes his way, fluttering to and fro, landing on a nearby planter and chirping to me with his face tilting. He is letting me know he has seen me, and I love every moment of it.

My children are also skeptical about this. They, too, say, "Oh, Mom, we know." They are brushing me off in a sweet way. But I cannot help it. When I hear Cardinal praising, I get exited. I get all squirmy and ask my family once again, "Hey, don't you hear it?" I can't believe you're not hearing what I hear. It's as clear as day: "PRAISE ... PRAISE ... PRAISE YOU!" But they don't hear it.

Unfortunately, for the past ten years this is what my family and friends have had to deal with. Yes, I must admit, I did put a few of my recordings of the beautiful praise song on social media. I was hoping someone else would hear this beautiful melody coming straight from the heavens. I wasn't at all concerned about what someone might think of me. I just didn't want others to miss out on something so beautiful.

Once I was asked if was able to understand any other sound of God's creation. My answer to that was, "No, I can't." Currently I have been limited to hearing only cardinals. But I am quite happy with that, for it gives me overwhelming joy.

Let me brag on how good Daddy is! Daddy, in all His mercy, came to my rescue and made a way to confirm that I had not lost it after all (I knew I hadn't). Yes, He did.

You might ask, "Why would God do such a thing?" Well, because He's my Daddy. Maybe He decided to reveal that this was a possibility and not just for me. I myself did not need any convincing. He may have wanted to reveal this truth to show others that I was not the only one whose ears are open to the supernatural realm. But this evidence didn't come until five years later.

Five years went by. One night my husband and I were ordering a certain book by a well-known psalmist. On his web page, he was offering a bundle special. The second book was not from him per say, but it was part of the bundle. It was by an artist he had worked with in the past. The title of the second book caught my attention in a big way, and my eyes locked onto it. I knew Daddy had placed that book in front of me for a reason, and I placed an order for the two books.

When the books arrived, I put a claim on that one. I could not wait to dissect it. I wanted to read what this man was proclaiming he knew. He acknowledged that he had experienced hearing certain creation sounds as well. Daddy had come to my rescue.

This man spoke about his encounters, hearing praises from many voices of creation. He was not limited to just Cardinal. I can promise you this book was my defender. I had proof that I was not a nutcase. The name of the book was *Heaven's Symphony: Your Invitation to Unlocking Divine Encounters Through Worship,*[1] and it was written by Steve Swanson. If your curiosity kicks in, you may just want to read it for yourself.

I'm telling you it's true, and since then, I have come across others proclaiming the very same thing. You maybe the next!

---

1. Shippensburg, PA, Destiny Image: 2015

My eighth unaware encounter with the courts of Heaven was this:

This is one of those encounters where Daddy came to encounter me from His heavenly courts. He gave me a gift that points right back to Him. It was the opening of my spiritual ears that I may hear the supernatural realm of His creation praising Him. In all essence, in all these years, Daddy has been allowing me to step into His courts, allowing me to partake of this heavenly melody that belongs to Him alone.

I believe this is why, when the melody starts, it demands my full attention. Immediately I think on God, for out of the vocals of Cardinal, I hear His high praises. And, as I gaze upon Cardinal, I am reminded of Jesus, my precious Savior who bled and died for me.

Prior to this, I had never heard the song of creation, which is not a distant melody to Daddy. This melody has been resounding in His courts since the beginning of time. He hears all creation praising Him.

All I know is that I long to hear Cardinal sing his praise song to God his maker—"PRAISE

... PRAISE ... PRAISE YOU!" I never get tired of it. It is truly captivating. There are no words to fully describe it. If time lapse and my surroundings become quiet, I long to hear that melody once again.

Daddy, being such a faithful and loving Father, opens the heavens and lets me in. Once again, I hear Cardinal serenading Him with his praise, as he joins in with Heaven's symphony, the melody of "PRAISE ... PRAISE ... PRAISE YOU!"

> *Then I heard every creature in Heaven and on earth and under the earth and on the sea, and all that is in them, saying:*
> *"To Him who sits on the throne and to the Lamb*
> *be praise and honor and glory and power, for ever and ever."* Revelation 5:13

> *Let everything that has breath praise the* LORD. Psalm 150:6

CHAPTER 11

My Ninth Unaware Encounter
(A CASE AGAINST ME?)

In this ninth encounter, I found myself coming face to face with a real opponent and literally fighting for my life. This adversary somehow and someway was plotting a case against me. It appeared in the natural that he had figured a way to destroy me and bring me to ruin.

Although I knew I had the Word of God, and it was my defender, the wiles of the enemy keep coming. I asked, "What was the evidence he was using against me? What was giving him the right to accuse me—if there was any right?

I would have lost heart, unless I had believed

That I would see the goodness of the
LORD
In the land of the living.
                    Psalm 27:13, NKJV

The thief does not come expect to steal,
and to kill, and to destroy. I have come
that they may have life, and that they
may have it more abundantly.
                    John 10:10, NKJV

At this point in my life, I experienced a rude awaking to the truth that we cannot do anything in and of ourselves in this life unless the Lord enables it. I was suddenly hurled into a realm where I was losing the ability to function in life as I had before. It was atrocious in every way.

For myself, it was like having a rug pulled out from under me, and I was left undone. The spiral of events was causing me to lose my sense of purpose and my independence in life and become detached from the world I had known so well.

My Ninth Unaware Encounter

I had always been a giver and not a taker. Serving others came naturally to me. In this season of my life, I was not able to give and be a servant that others could depend on. To tell the truth, I couldn't even take care of myself.

As time passed, I recalled a morning when this thought came to mind:

"If I should ever come to a place in my life, that I would wake up and not remember my surroundings, what would my last worship look like? Would my last worship to God have been of great passion to the One I love?"

This was how debilitating the situation was at the moment. Let's be real. I'm sure you have come to this place in your own life at one time or another, perhaps in a different way. Up to then, I had operated in my own strength and abilities, just as healthy and vibrant people do. I can boldly say that as you wake, you have absolutely no idea what it means not to be able to function outside of yourself. There is no reason for you to, for everything in your world is normal.

I had been there all my life as well and never gave it a second thought. We rise as the morning sun peeks into our rooms. We put our feet on the floor, and we get moving. That's just what we do. That's how life is without hindrances.

Having an abundance of money in life is considered a big blessing. It is exciting to have extra, I must agree. But if your health is gone, you won't have the time or energy to enjoy what money can bring. Health outweighs wealth any day. It is the better blessing. It is health that gives us the ability to produce wealth.

Prior to this rude awaking, I was known as the Energizer Bunny. From the moment I awoke to the time I laid my head down at night, I was moving nonstop. Multi-tasking was my specialty, wearing many hats, as they say.

Creativity was a gift I had inherited from my mom. I quilted, sewed, crafted, made flower beds and gardens, cultivated compost bins, and eventually had a greenhouse to play in. My yard was my dominion, and manicuring it was my pleasure. This pattern followed within the walls of my home. My family never went without a meal or clean clothing. They were the priority on my list. God gave me the grace, and I was able to walk in the ease of it all.

My capabilities had not run dry yet. A few years after giving Jesus my life, I learned sign language. I feel it is proper to say it was Holy Spirit who taught me. I only went to class once. God has a wonderful sense of humor. He led a deaf person into our church the very next week. That was when Holy Spirit came in, directing my hands. It was a wonder to say the least. This ministry lasted for several years. God's capabilities are limitless; He is only looking for a vessel to work through.

Continuing to give God the glory, children's ministry was my first love. I taught for more than thirty-three years. At some point, I became Director of the entire program and was blessed to work with more than thirty teaches. What an honor! Together we accommodated six classes, four services per week. That was twenty-four classes in a week besides specialty classes. For our size church, that was quite impressive.

I mention the twenty-four classes for a reason. Being Director over the Children's Ministry, I knew every detail pertaining to every curriculum used in each class. That was a lot of information stored in my brain, and I was running full throttle with it. During this time in my life, my spreadsheet included anything pertaining to children's ministry, the children's drama, choir, puppetry, Vacation Bible School, and more. During that time, I also wrote a children's curriculum on the Armor of God, as well as revising a few curriculums we had already been using.

Believe it or not, with all of this going on, once a week I would go clean a lady's house. When I began working for her, she had a child under the age of three. I cleaned for her up to the time her daughter started college. When they moved from house to house, I accompanied them. When they made their last move, 103 miles away, I assisted them there for a while as well. They were a great blessing to me.

Let me take it a little further. My pastor's wife had a bright idea. She approached the Daycare director and myself and said, "Since both of you need drivers to tote you around for your outings, I figured maybe it was a good idea for you to get your own CDL license. Then you can drive yourselves around." I did just that, but I was not comfortable driving the children just yet. I really didn't have that many hours under my belt, so to speak. Especially if I were to drive the 393 miles to Columbus, Texas for summer camp meeting.

I decided to drive part time for our local schools so I could become more acquainted with handling buses. Little did I know that learning mechanic's skills came with the territory. In the end, I drove seventeen years full-time for the school board. God blessed that journey, and it became another out-reach ministry for children. I loved it and became a part of many families.

It was a funny sight for me to drive up to the church office in my mini-bus on the days I worked there as well. (I had a mini-bus for a mini-route in between my big routes.)

During the latter years of my big bus career, I became my younger sister's caregiver. She had been diagnosed with leukemia a few years before. In the last year of her life, I had her moved in with me, so I could care for her. Eventually I had to take sick leave from work on her behalf.

She was scheduled for a bone marrow transplant at M.D. Anderson Hospital in Houston, Texas. We were there four months before I had to fly her back home. The transplant was unsuccessful. We, as a family, were given an additional eight days with her before she went home to be with the Lord.

My dad was a pastor at the time and had a church in the country. I had not been led to attend his church, but Lisa, my sister, was part of his ministry. Since she was living with me for the last year of her life, our whole family also attended church there.

My Ninth Unaware Encounter

Later, after Lisa passed away, I remained and became heavily involved with that ministry. Again, I spread my wings and dove right back into children's ministry and now found myself as the church secretary as well. Now I was wearing a new hat.

You may be wondering why I am giving you my life story. Is this relevant at all? This is not to exalt me. Many of these abilities that I walked in I had never once foreseen as a possibility for myself. God is the One who has made deposits within us. He has given us capabilities in areas that He desired for us to walk in. The telling of my story is only to prove a matter in conjunction to this case being built against me.

I am reminded of an episode with my neurologist. How do you explain to another all your capabilities when they don't know the real you? They don't know how far you have fallen from your own self. That was the reason I have shared my life with you.

I remember going into the neurologist's office one day, frustrated because it was too difficult to explain what was happening in my brain. There were days when I couldn't put forward one more thought or even read my mail (which was very important at the time). It was debilitating, to say the least. My brain could not handle it.

Does this sound like the me who you just read about in the previous paragraphs? No, it was not! I remember slamming down my life before him, laying out photos of the more than forty quilts I had made, my plaque from graduating Bible school for two years with a 4.0 average, along with the curriculum I wrote and so much other things. He needed to know that the person sitting in his office was not the real me.

During one office visit, as I was standing up for myself, knowing I was not going crazy, nurses came running in. They wanted me to sign a paper giving them consent to send me to the looney house. I knew exactly what was happening.

I became so frustrated with testings giving only partial information, and what was really there was not being addressed. I became known as the non-compliant patient, a failure for not taking my prescribe medicines. I was not going into fall in that trap. Those meds were strong, and I could have easily become dependent upon many of them. Those were only Band-Aids for a matter they could not diagnose. That was not the way this issue was to be resolved.

During office visits, we were allowed only a few minutes with the doctors. If truth be told, I was tired of my time being spent in other conversations, like joking, and not on why I was there. I was crying out for answers. I was tired of praying away symptoms. I knew I needed to get to the source so it could be severed at the root, and I was not getting that answer. This went on for years.

Eventually, I found myself having to repent a time or two. Bitterness was lurking, knocking at my door. I knew of others who had experienced health issues, and they were healed. How nice for them to move on with life and not be bothered by their thorn in the flesh again! I wanted to be in that category as well. Their healings may have come by way of a new knee, or a stint, or just as simple as taking in a little sugar, and all was made well. How was I to go on my merry way in my situation?

Have you ever heard of someone getting a new brain? I needed a new one so that I could function in life, but that didn't seem to be an option.

During all this time it seemed like the prosecutor's case was mounting against me. I was on trial, and it was intense. I felt like a prisoner already, although I had not yet been sentenced.

When I said earlier that I was able to mul-titask, I wasn't joking. I had never been a couch potato. I had always made good use of my time. I was highly blessed by God. He gave me great health. I had absolutely no issue in that department ever before ... until this day came.

During the early summer of 2011, my face began going numb from time to time, but I didn't think it was a big deal. My left arm and leg would do the same. Still, this didn't hinder my ability to function normally. I passed it off as a fluke situation.

My Ninth Unaware Encounter

Then came 2013. We were two weeks shy of the ending of the school year and getting ready for summer break. By this time, I was driving a bus for handicapped children and had just a few of them and an aide.

On this certain evening, I was en route, delivering my children for the day, when suddenly I lost all data in my brain for the next stop. Where was my next stop? I could not bring up anything familiar. There was nothing to draw from. My brain was completely blank as to the location of that stop or its surroundings, such as neighborhoods, streets, or stores. I knew who I was, and I knew everyone I had onboard, but it was only with the help of my aide that I was able to deliver the rest of the children safely to their homes.

By the end of two weeks, there was a major shifting taking place within me. I didn't know what was going on, and I was beginning to have bouts of anxiety that were very foreign to me. That onslaught continued until May 24, 2017. That is when God delivered me from anxiety. Hallelujah!

With so much going on in my body in so many ways, it was as if I had gotten plugged into a circuit box and left there to fry. It was really time for school to end. Sad to say, I had to retire from driving the bus. There was no way to pass my physical for the following year.

From 2013 until 2017, I underwent multiple MRIs. I went from being extremely energetic to seeing myself literally out of commission. At the beginning of this season, I was debilitated seven months with a fatigue that was truly from the pit of Hell. I seemed like a person who had been left for dead.

I had lost my independence, as I said earlier, and hated every minute of it. Driving becoming impossible with the swirling going on in my head. Besides, on several occasions I passed out without warning. Those were likely mini-strokes. My MRI scans revealed that I had suffered mini-strokes that had gone unnoticed, even by me.

On those occasions, my husband carried me to bed and prayed over me. Later,

I would wake up and seem to be okay. Everything that was taking place in my body scientifically pointed to Multiple Sclerosis. Eventually, I underwent a spinal tap, but it came back negative. Praise God for that! But the relapses kept coming, and it was my brain that was suffering the most.

Eventually, I was fed up with this trial. The results of a PET Scan came back the same as the many MRIs. Findings were suggestive of an Alzheimers-type dementia pattern. Deep within my right frontal lobe white matter there was atrophy. This damage would be more than likely due to demyelination, which is caused by MS, ischemia, or hypertension (which I did not relate to).

Strangely, in all those years, my doctor was very vague about the MRI results. It seemed as if I was throwing money to the wind. He really would not give me a report on them. He would say, "Overall, it's not so bad."

But my family doctor who first sent me for an MRI said my brain was lit up like a Christmas tree. There were many dots on it, and they didn't belong there.

I was told by a doctor I saw in New York that my brain speed was extremely slow. Looking at my results suggested that I needed to be in a nursing home. Thankfully, he agreed with me that I was not the person my test results said I was.

I thanked God for my good days, but I was exhausted with praying the symptoms away. I knew I had to get to the root of the problem. I was so done with formulas 1, 2, and 3, along with formulas A, B, and C. I was at the mercy of God.

My Ninth Unaware Encounter

In this, my ninth encounter with the courts of Heaven, I was in desperate need of a Defense Attorney.

Being a Christian, I knew the importance of guarding my heart and my life, not giving the enemy any entry point where he could cause havoc. Up to this point, I understood that I was under an attack, but it was only an attack of the enemy. I did not consider it as a case against me.

I knew I was going through a trial, but like you, I often went through trials. With that understanding, I did everything I knew to do to end the madness.

What I did not envision was that this case was literally being presented in the courts of Heaven before my Father. It was a case the prosecutor had built against me that I did not envision. I did not know what avenue he, the enemy, was using against me, if there were any, or what he was presenting before God that gave him the legal right to do this to me. As Holy Spirit unveiled this truth, I began to look in God's Word at the various avenues that might be giving him this right.

Who knows, maybe this was how Job felt. With all these afflictions, was the accuser waiting for me to curse God in my time of affliction or to see if I would remain faithful to Daddy God?

Another possible scenario may have been that the enemy had a legal accusation against me that I was not aware of. Was he using it against me in the courts of Heaven to where God could not release my healing? I knew I had to examine my heart and repent for whatever might be hidden.

On the other hand, maybe it was like Daniel's situation. Was my situation following the same pattern as his? He prayed and prayed just as I had, but his answer didn't come until later. We do know that his prayers got answered, but the answer was delayed because of spiritual warfare against them.

I had a few people say to me that maybe this was a spirit of infirmity. Or maybe it was a squatter who needed evicting from God's property. All I know is that I had done all I knew to do, and it had not left me yet.

In my weakness, I kept the Word of God before me. I stood my ground, knowing who I was in Christ, knowing that His Word overrode all that I was going through. I may not have considered it all joy, going through this fiery trial, but I was not going down without a fight. The conclusion to this madness was apparent: I needed a good defense lawyer to help me.

CHAPTER 12

My Tenth Unaware Encounter
(THE THRONE OF GRACE)

Have you ever read a book or watched a movie, only to realize you were being taken in by a story within a story? Having a subplot in which the side story runs parallel to the main plot can be quite surprising. It is a wonder how something so complex can become intertwined into one.

Coincidentally this was a nugget Holy Spirit revealed to me concerning this chapter. He didn't share this when He first unveiled my unaware encounters with the courts. Instead, He surprised me with this gem when I was looking over my writings.

I knew every single detail of my story pertaining to this specific timing in my life and was able to cross every t and dot every i. But never once had I considered this encounter to be Part 2 of my storyline, my journey. To think I had a story within a story would have seemed absurd to me at the time.

Surprisingly, several years have come and gone since I walked this journey, only to find out that my story did not begin where I thought it had. There was a chief part that existed before.

In all reality, that chief part of my story is the pivotal point. That was the little gem Holy Spirit surprised me with. It was that hidden part which led me into the latter encounters that I was able to explain so well.

Back in January, when Holy Spirit popped in saying, "Hey, I have something to tell you. You have had unaware encounters with the courts of Heaven. Let me show you," He was not kidding.

When He said my encounters had started with this little gem, I can promise you I did not see myself standing where He saw me. This was the part of my story that did not exist as far as I was concerned.

To be honest, I didn't realize I had even

caught Holy Spirit's attention on that dreadful day. It was over time that I saw He was moving in my life and gently led me to a place I never had heard of or been before. That is the part of my story I knew beyond a shadow of a doubt. Shockingly, my inspirational and heartfelt journey ends up being my story within the story. It was the Part 2 of my chronicles.

With that in mind, I want to stir your curiosity of where I journeyed to. The place I went to is not your prime choice location for vacationing. We would never consider such a destination, but it was the dwelling place Holy Spirit led me to for refreshing in my time of need. It has become, by far, the most beautiful place I have ever been.

Nevertheless, I won't begin there just yet, for, as you can see, I didn't know this place existed. It has, however, an appointed time in my story. Let me take you on my journey as it unfolded in my time sequence.

It was the Spring of 2017, mid-mornng on a beautiful Saturday. My goal was to prepare lunch for my husband and myself. While doing so, I was listening to an arrangement of songs I call my "prayer songs." The Lord led me to each one of them. During my journey, He said, "These are songs of deliverance. These are songs you will be prophesying your promises from." Ironically, later, in 2018, a song came out called just that.

In the meantime, the health issues were still showing their faces. I could say much about what was happening, but my brain feeling swollen was one huge issue. It seemed that at any given moment it might explode.

This day was no different, but even though fiery attacks were coming from every direction, I still rose to encourage myself, only later to find myself under an onslaught that eventually brought me to my knees. I was done. The intensity of this warfare rose to a level I had not thought was possible. In all reality, it was happening, and I despised every minute of it.

I didn't want to identify or be associated with being weak. I had always been an independent woman in a healthy way. Now cooking, which had always been a passion of mine, became an impossible task that day. Anyone knowing me knows I could cook with my eyes closed.

Once again, I was experiencing the same trauma as on the bus, losing data, along with all the other attacks hitting me simultaneously.

I could not recollect what to do next, as I gazed into the pot sitting on my stove. I didn't know why those diced vegetables were sitting on the cutting board. Nothing that was in my view was making any sense to me. I remember watching my hands shaking and feeling my brain swirling within me. I was standing in total blankness.

The longer I stood over the food the more intense the problem got. I knew I was not able to finish cooking, and I broke, falling to the floor right there in my kitchen. I was scorched by the ambush. I bust into sobbing and screamed from the top of my lungs with a certainty that the whole world could hear me.

I also bellowed out to God, "I cannot do this anymore. If I cannot function in this life as I did before, get me out of this body and bring me home. Just bring me home!"

I was so done with this life. My cry in that moment was not a cry for help; it was more of a defeated surrender. I quit!

I wish I could tell you that I had a glorious encounter with God that day, but no. It was the same as when I gave Him my life. There were no frills or thrills.

Eventually I lifted my seemingly-lifeless body from the floor, stood to my feet, washed my face, and that was that ... or so I thought.

In those moments, I felt as though the heavens were brass. It seemed impossible that my voice could leave the earth and make its way to Heaven.

By all accounts, my journey began when I fell at the altar in my kitchen. I said I didn't have an encounter with Daddy. There was nothing notable that I was able to give an account of. But in time, as I looked back, something beautiful in the Spirit had taken place.

Soon after that I came across a picture. There is that lovely word *picture* again. As I gazed upon that photo, I saw myself in it. In this picture, a man is facing down, lying in the rain. His body is drenched. I see a dove is present. The dove has taken hold of the back of the man's shirt, and with his gentle grip, he begins to lift the man up from the ground. As the dove lifts the man's lifeless body, his arms and legs hang limp. Around the picture it reads: "WHEN YOU WANT TO GIVE UP, BUT HOLY SPIRIT LIFTS YOU UP."

Holy Spirit knew this picture would minister to my weary soul, and He used it to say, "Hey, this is what I have come to do for you too." He gently began lifting me up and leading me on a journey of recovery. It took days before I realized what He had orchestrated. One thing was sure: as time passed, I was being nursed back to health

This was proven more and more as days went by. I did have a loving Daddy who wanted to meet my needs. In that moment, as I had cried out to God, seriously wanting Him to take me home. I was tired of the trauma my body had been under. My flesh and my mind had called it quits. Although my cry came from my innermost being on that dreadful day, my spirit knew that my life here was not ye finished.

Looking back, I see how the Lord counseled me little by little. The first thing Holy Spirit impressed upon me was Psalm 91:1-2:

> *He that dwelleth in the secret place of the most High shall abide under the shadow of the Almighty. I will say of the LORD, He is my refuge and my fortress: my God, in him will I trust."* (KJV)

Within a week or two of meditating on these scriptures, Holy Spirit highlighted the words *dwell* and *abide*. Apparently, I had been overlooking them. Me capturing their meanings was of upmost importance to Him. He wanted to take me deeper and that He did.

Throughout my Christian life I enjoyed when ministers expanded word meanings from the Hebrew or Greek. Although I had done it a time or two myself, it was not my normal study habit. I can't say that any-more. The Spirit now opened my world to dig into the Hebrew and Greek meanings of words.

Taking everything at face value was no more. I wanted to dissect words to the point of their origins, and this part of my journey keeps growing, even as I write.

With that in mind, let us investigate the Hebrew meaning of *dwell*.

> *Dwell*: *Bible Tool Greek/Hebrew Definitions Strong's Concordance* #3427: *yashab*, "to sit down, to remain, to settle, to marry; to abide, habitation, make to keep house, marry."

Holy Spirit is a great Counselor. First, He guided me with baby steps to study the words coming from their Hebrew meaning. Then He led me to a more challenging and somewhat complex study of their mean-ings. This was seen through the lens of the Hebrew alphabet, dissecting each letter and its meaning to the Hebrew word.

Once again, Holy Spirit led me to a woman I had never heard of before. She was Mary Ellen Wright. She had an in-depth study of Psalm 91 in this fashion, and this has taken my studying to a whole new level.

Holy Spirit opened my understanding to the fact that there are hidden secrets and truths in the Hebrew alphabet. Every Hebrew letter has a picture, a number value, and meaning that is tied to it. As I looked at each letter and its vast meanings, He had me—hook, line, and sinker—and suddenly I was drawn to view God's Word through this new lens as well.

Looking at *"He who dwells"* by breaking it down with the Hebrew alphabet and the meaning, as seen in Mary Ellen Wright's study, it would read like this:

He who dwells: He who moves in permanently – trusting in God and obeying him, will experience the activation of His hand of power, His Holy Spirit, consuming with His fire all that destroys or tries to invade or keep us from His house.

Now that is shedding light on the Word, wouldn't you say?

Now for the word *abides*:

> *Bible Tools Strong's Greek Concordance* #3306: *meno*, "*t*o stay (in a given place, state, relation or expectancy):—abide, continue, dwell, endure, be present, remain, stand, tarry (for)." *Biblehub.com Strong's Concordance* #3885 *luwn*, definition: "to lodge, pass the night, abide."

This is where Holy Spirit had me for the next year and a half, 24/7—literally.

So, yes, the studying of these words for my life at that present moment meant that I had moved permanently into the presence of Daddy God, where Holy Spirt was destroying everything that was coming against me. I now found myself sitting at the feet of Jesus continually. I was totally content with that!

During this time, I could have cared less about anything going on around me, and that was a big deal. You must understand: before this encounter, I was alone for a lengthy period of time, feeling that I had been missing out on life. It was not that I wanted to. I recall anger rising within me. No longer surrounded by people as I once had been, my illness was stripping my life right down to the core, and I hated it.

I lost my job, and going anywhere became intolerable. Normal activity around me was hard to bear. What had once been a normal unconscious effort to process became a nightmare. Driving myself around, as I always had, was now out of the question. My disorientation was off the chart.

Losing my independence left me at the mercy of my husband, my daughter, a very close friend, and my parents at times. They were the ones who tended to me. I cannot believe I just wrote those words about myself, that I needed someone to tend to me. This makes me pause for a moment and say, "Thank You, Daddy. Thank You for not leaving me in that state of being. Glory! Hallelujah!

Now I found myself coming back to life again. The anger of not being social or going places began to fade away in the light of where Holy Spirit was taking me. I was content, just basking in God's presence. Basking in His Word, sitting at the feet of Jesus, was all I looked forward to. It was effortless.

Although I looked forward to being with them, they were the ones pursuing me. I was overwhelmed by the treasures they would surprise me with.

At the beginning of this journey, Holy Spirit introduced me to a book. It was *The Prayer of Protection: Living Fearlessly in Dangerous Times* by Joseph Prince.[2] Once I opened it, I was not able to put it down. It was a tool that would further me on my journey. Holy Spirit had just given me the first two verses from Psalm 91 to meditate on. By giving myself to the reading of this book I discovered something. I saw that Psalm 91 went deeper than God's provision to protect us through life's circumstances. It does that, but this was not what I was

2. New York, NY (Faith Words: 2017)

receiving from Holy Spirit for myself. This book spoke volumes on intimacy with the Father, Son, and Holy Spirit. That was what I was getting out of it, being ever so intimate with them.

Looking ahead, two years later, the Bible study I held in my home was centered around this book but not limited to it. The study's main focus was becoming intimate with the Trinity. In due time, I ended up with a three-inch binder of wonders of where Holy Spirit had led me.

Who would have ever thought it was possible for me to sit and take in so much? This was a God thing! I could write a book on just the nuggets He gave me during this time.

Continuing in my journey, I would get caught up in His presence and lose track of time. I know Holy Spirit took care of that as well. Eventually, in the nick of time, He would make it known that it was time to prepare my husband's meal. I didn't need a physical meal. I was staying full from God's Word and His presence.

You may be asking yourself, "When will she tell us about the place Holy Spirit took her to?" I haven't forgotten. You may not have realized it, but we have already stepped into the timeline of my story to that destination. Just like you, I was unaware of it as well. It was about this time in my journey when Holy Spirit unfolded this truth. He introduced me to my destination, which is called Midbar.

This supernatural encounter was the place He brought me to. It was the place to experience intimacy with Daddy and with Jesus, the Lover of my soul. From the time Holy Spirit gently lifted me from my kitchen floor, He had my luggage already packed. He placed it in my hand and transported me to Midbar. My time sitting at their feet during that year and a half was a spiritual investment that brought me back to life.

I enjoyed the encounters in which Holy Spirit led me to quotes from others, from scriptures and studies pertaining to Midbar and more, revelations and insights to areas of His Word that I never given thought of before, nor even imagined. His itinerary had it all, and it was tailored just for me. He planned out this vacation "to the T," as they say.

During this time, I was basking in this oasis that provided me refuge and relief. I had springs of living water flowing in me and through me. I must compliment Holy Spirit for taking me to such a place. He was navigating my studies like He never had before, and I was thanking Him for the work He had done in my life during my journey to Midbar.

You may have been like me. I had never heard of such a place. Let me unfold its meaning to you so you can see it for yourself. It is quite interesting, complex, I must agree, but oh so interesting.

In Hebrew, the word *Midbar* in the *Bible Tools Strong's Concordance* #4057 is defined as "**speech, wilderness**."

Brown Driver-Briggs Hebrew Lexicon: Midbar,

"1) **wilderness**

2) **mouth** 2a) **mouth** (as an organ of speech)."

Biblehub.com *NAS Exhaustive Concordance* #4057 states that the word origin for **Midbar** comes from the Hebrew word **dabar**.

Its definition is *"mouth."*

Also, *Biblehub.com NAS Exhaustive Concordance* #4057b states the word origin for **midbar** comes from the Hebrew word *"dabar."*

Its definition means *"wilderness."*

Now *dabar*, according to *Bible Tools Strong's Concordance* #1697 can also be defined as meaning "**words, to speak.**"

The essence of studying words in their original meanings may seem a bit challenging, but it is quite rewarding and exciting. Hang tight! These meanings of *midbar* and *dabar* come together in a beautiful way.

Now knowing the meaning of midbar, who in their right mind would want to vacation in a dry, deserted, desert or journey through an area that was only wilderness? As I said at the beginning of this chapter, being in the wilderness is not our prime choice place for vacationing.

Midbar is desolate. There are no main attractions there. As far as you can see, there is nothing in sight, absolutely nothing to grab your attention. In this place, you are not being pulled to and fro. Once again, in this place, there are no distractions of any kind. Oh, but in this place called wilderness there is a voice that speaks. It is in this beautiful place where all you hear is the Word of God.

This is where the meanings of these two words come together. You may not realize it at first, but this is the place of separation unto God. This is the place of preparation, a place where He is preparing you for something greater. This is the place of revelation where He unfolds His secrets and His hidden truths.

This destination is a place we should all hunger and thirst for. When you have been brought there supernaturally, you never feel the need to leave. Seconds turn into minutes, that leads to hours, days and weeks that lead to months. In my case, it was a whole year and a half, and yet it was so easy to sit and linger with Daddy God and never feel like it was time to move on to something else.

I know that we have other obligations in life. I'm just saying that when Holy Spirit orchestrates this trip for you, He will take care of everything else.

Do you recall biblical stories of others who were led into the wilderness? We have read time and again of Moses, Abraham, Elijah, and Jesus Himself entering this place. We have all read that it was in this place where they heard the voice of God in a unique way. This is the place where God speaks to strengthen, guide, and encourage us.

Midbar has much to offer us. It is a place of hidden treasures, a place you walk away from knowing that God has spoken secrets and hidden truths of His Word to you.

My time in Midbar was far from being dry and deserted; it was a journey of God's wooing me into His inner courts. It was during this time that He revealed to me the woman at the well as she appears in the Scriptures. It was of utmost importance to Him that I would connect with her. He led me to her name, Photini, according to historical findings. I was beside myself with her story and wanted everyone to know her name.

This woman had always been simply "the woman at the well" for the past forty years of my Christian life. Never once had I heard her name spoken by any minister.

Two years later, after going through all this, Holy Spirit blessed me through a Christian program. The program was about this very woman and her time at the well meeting Jesus. It began with her husband calling her name, Photini.

I was blown away to finally hear someone in Christian circles acknowledging the woman by name, and I was able to connect with her. We were two women who had been scorched through life's circumstances. On a path that seemed dry and lonely, we were also two women who had been met by Jesus and, after having that encounter, we were both filled with rivers of living water. Those rivers rose up within us, bursting forth, bubbling up, and spilling over onto others. I had received a double dose since having Holy Spirit living in me.

From that time on, I found myself constantly singing in the Spirit, as well as singing in English whatever worship song Holy Spirit place on my tongue. It was free-flowing and was not limited to my private time. It was from the moment I opened my eyes to the time I closed them. It was the same for praying. I was experiencing times of refreshing, and my days were filled with joy. I felt I once again had a future to look forward to.

Considering how God created our bodies, we must acknowledge that we were made from the dust of the ground. I had never compared myself to a desert. In all reality, however, if our body lacks the water it needs, eventually it will dry up and die, and we will become like a barren desert where life is no longer a productive factor.

It is the same for our soul. Going through trials has its way of leaving us dry or parched. We need the refreshing rains, the living waters from the Word of God to come and restore life to us once again.

I mentioned in a previous chapter that I was tired of formula 1, 2, and 3 or formula A, B, and C. I didn't know at the time that when I spoke those words it became the best decision I had ever made. Why? Because I was letting God out of the box I had placed Him in. This opened a new avenue for Him to minister life to me in a fresh new way.

This avenue did not look familiar, but it has been most rewarding. The people, the studies, and the music all played a vital role in my journey. I didn't run from the unfamiliar just because I had never heard of these people, these songs, or these newfound words. No, I simply flowed in the gentle rivers of where Holy Spirit led me.

So, let me just say: if you find yourself in the wilderness in an unfamiliar place, embrace it. Why? Because it's not the end. God sees the end from the beginning:

> *I took care of you in the wilderness,*
> *in that dry and thirsty land.*
> Hosea 13:5, NLT

My Tenth Unaware Encounter

*It was I who knew you in the wilderness,
in the land of drought.* (ESV)

In life, you may find yourself in a drought where no doctor, no spouse, and not even a friend can fully understand your situation. They cannot fathom what is going on inside of you, and therefore, they don't know how to help you. You feel alone in this dry and weary land, but the God you serve sees you. He knows you, and He alone knows how to care for you. He alone will water you in that dry and scorched land. He will lead you to refreshing waters.

God is not a respecter of persons. What He has been doing for me He will certainly do for you too. During my journey, He led me to Isaiah 35. This was Daddy's way of encouraging me that this wilderness would break forth in my favor. Daddy has a way with me, just like He does with you, to get our attention. With me, He singles out a word and causes it to stand out. Here in this passage, He does that.

There are many words here that I could highlight. I will emphasize a few, but I would suggest that you just claim this entire passage for yourself. That's what I have done. The lesson is entitled **The Joy of the Redeemed:**

*THE DESERT AND THE PARCHED
LAND WILL BE GLAD;
THE WILDERNESS WILL REJOICE
AND BLOSSOM.*
*Like the crocus, it will burst into bloom;
it will rejoice greatly and shout for joy.
The glory of Lebanon will be given to it,
the splendor of Carmel and Sharon,
they will see the glory of the* LORD,
the splendor of our God.

*Strengthen the feeble hands,
steady the knees that give way;
say to those with fearful hearts,
"Be strong, do not fear;
your God will come,
he will come with vengeance,
with divine retribution
 he will come to save you.*

*Then will the eyes of the blind be opened
and the ears of the deaf unstopped.
Then will the lame leap like a deer,
and the mute tongue shout for joy.*
***WATER WILL GUSH FORTH IN
THE WILDERNESS
AND STREAMS IN THE DESERT.
THE BURNING SAND WILL BE-
COME A POOL,
THE THIRSTY GROUND BUB-
BLING SPRINGS.***
*In the haunts where jackals once lay,
grass and reeds and papyrus will grow.*

***AND A HIGHWAY WILL BE THERE;
IT WILL BE CALLED THE WAY OF
HOLINESS;
IT WILL BE FOR THOSE WHO
WALK ON THAT WAY.***
*The unclean will not journey on it;
wicked fools will not go about on it.
No lion will be there,
nor any ravenous beast;
they will not be found there.*
BUT ONLY THE REDEEMED WILL

WALK THERE,
AND THOSE THE LORD HAS RES-
CUED WILL RETURN.
THEY WILL ENTER ZION WITH
SINGING;
EVERLASTING JOY WILL CROWN
THEIR HEADS.
GLADNESS AND JOY WILL OVER-
TAKE THEM,
AND SORROW AND SIGHING
WILL FLEE AWAY.   Isaiah 35:1-10
(Emphasis Mine)

Previously I said that Holy Spirit strategically orchestrated people in my life whom I never heard of, and He did it for my betterment. He had a purpose for placing them right in front of me.

First, it was Elizabeth Nixon, whom He used to introduced me to what are called "the courts of Heaven." This was to reveal to me my personal encounters with those courts.

Secondly, he used Gretchen Mure Rodriguez, a well-known author. She has also written alongside Brian Simmons. God's purpose for introducing me to her was to reaffirm that I had been to this place called Midbar, along with the detailed facts of where it had led me to and what I had gained from it.

Gretchen and I were not considered "friends" on a peculiar social-media site, and prior to this, there had been no requests ever made between the two of us. Her name was, as they say, "Greek to me." But this was the platform Holy Spirit used so that I could gaze upon a beautiful quote of hers. It reads:

"THE WILDERNESS THAT STRIPPED ME BARE BECAME MY BEAUTIFUL VICTORY!"

Those words radiated down to my very core. This is what I had been walking in over time, having been stripped of everything I had known, from everything I was familiar with. Somehow, by the grace of God, I had made it through. I finally arrived in victory, despite the facts of my journey and all I had gone through. I had been at a loss for words to describe what had taken place. Holy Spirit allowed me to see it from someone else's point of view. Those words are beautiful to my spirit, soul, and body.

During my journey to Midbar, Holy Spirit opened the realm of Hebrew worship to me as well. Once again, He led me to people I had no knowledge of. Among them, I have a few choice favorites: Joshua Aaron, Paul Wilbur, Aaron Shust, and Sarah Liberman. Sitting under the anointing of Hebrew worship, I am learning to sing and understand words in that language. I am now able to express my song, "How Great Is Our God," to Him in Hebrew.

Before I go on, can you see the working of Holy Spirit in my life? Just chapters before, I stated that many times I was not even able to read my mail. I was not able to put another word or thought in my brain. It would become overloaded, which led to many days in bed, shutting out the world, shutting down my brain so it could somehow reboot for a later day. Look what Holy Spirit has already done in me. I don't want you to pass it up. I am being healed on this journey!

At some point, Holy Spirit gave me a scripture to hold on to, and I have been wanting to stand up and testify what God has done for me. This is the scripture He gave. I have it in nine different translations always before me in my home. As I wrote each one out, I applied my own name to it, so now they read:

By faith in the name of Jesus, [I, Emelda] whom you see and know <u>was made strong</u>. It is Jesus' name and the faith that comes through him that <u>has completely healed [me]</u>, as you can all see.

Acts 3:16, NIV
(Emphasis Mine)

And on the basis of faith in His name, it is the name of Jesus which <u>has strengthened [me</u>, Emelda], whom you see and know; and the faith which comes through Him has <u>given [me] this perfect health</u> in the presence of you all.

Acts 3:16, NASB
(Emphasis Mine)

Through faith in the name of Jesus, [I, Emelda], <u>was healed [in my brain</u> of any malfunctions], and you know how crippled [I] was before. Faith in Jesus' name <u>has healed [me]</u> before your very eyes. Acts 3:16, NLT
(Emphasis Mine)

And His name — by faith in His name — <u>has made [me, Emelda] strong</u>, whom you see and know, and the faith that is through Jesus has given [me] this <u>perfect health</u> in the presence of you all.
Acts 3:16, ESV
(Emphasis Mine)

And by faith in His name, [I, Emelda], whom you see and know, <u>He [Jesus] has restored and healed [my brain]</u>, and faith in His name has given [me] this health before you all. Acts 3:16, Aramaic
(Emphasis Mine)

And his name through faith in his name hath made [me, <u>Emelda] strong</u>, whom

210

ye see and know: yea, the faith which is by Him hath given [me] this perfect soundness in the presence of you all.

Acts 3:16, KJV
(Emphasis Mine)

[I] believe in the one named Jesus. Through his power alone [I, Emelda], whom you know, was healed [of every malfunction in my brain], as all of you saw.

Acts 3:16, GW
(Emphasis Mine)

It is His name—faith in that name being the condition—which has strengthened [me, Emelda], whom you behold and know; and the faith which He has given has made [me] sound and strong again, as you can all see.   Acts 3:16, WNT
(Emphasis Mine)

By faith in the name of Jesus, [I, Emelda], whom you see and know has been made strong. It is Jesus' name and the faith that comes through that has given

[me] *complete healing* in your pres-
ence.   Acts 3:16, BSB
                                    (Emphasis Mine)

You may not understand why I listed all
of these various translations of Acts 3:16.
For me, it was vital. It was my life that I was
warring for. This was a spoken *rhema* word
that God gave me to use in combatting the
evil one who was coming against my life.
God did this to assure me that, yes, I do win
this battle and I can stand firm in the victory
of His Word.

You see, during this time in Midbar, Holy
Spirit counseled me in a very beautiful way,
as I mentioned earlier. He had a habit of
placing fresh manna at my feet, knowing
that I would get excited about it. I didn't
have to go digging. It was as if He could not
wait to give me another gem. He knew that
such information was vital and that I needed
these revelations in my journey.

I came to notice that Holy Spirit has a pattern with me. He is still using it to this very
day. He leads me by studying a word or He

puts pictures or a number or a video in front of me which eventually ties me to a situation. This is His way of telling me, "Hey, I know right where you are and what is going on *around* you and *in* you."

I love it because I know it is Holy Spirit who is at work in the earth today. I know I have a relationship with Him as well as with my Daddy God and with Jesus, my Savior my soon-coming King, the Lover of my soul.

With that in mind, Holy Spirit placed before me an article by Rick Renner. It was called "You Have A Two-Edge Sword." It was to confirm that God had just given me the *rhema* word of Acts 3:16, and it was my sword for battle.

Formerly, I had understanding on God's Word concerning the sword of the Spirit, but not coming from the angle Rick was presenting it. How could I not share a portion of this with you here? You may find yourself seeing a deeper meaning of the Word, as I did. And, then again, this may be an old insight for you. The article is based on Hebrews 4:12:

For the word of God is quick, and powerful, and sharper than any TWO-EDGED SWORD, piercing even to the dividing asunder of the soul and spirit, and of the joints and marrow, and is a discerner of the thoughts and intents of the heart. (KJV)

(Emphasis Mine)

The article stated:

"What is the significance of the 'two-edge sword' referred to in Hebrews 4:12? If you start looking, you will find out this phrase regarding a 'two-edged sword' appears all over the New Testament, so it must be important. For instance, when the apostle John received his vision of Jesus on the isle of Patmos, he said, *'And he had in His right hand seven stars: and out of His mouth went a sharp two-edged sword: and His countenance was as the sun shineth in His strength'* (Revelation 1:16). Notice that this 'two-edged sword' came out of Jesus' mouth!

Why would Jesus have a sword in His mouth? Shouldn't the sword be in His hand?

"The phrase 'two-edged' is taken from the Greek word *distomos* and is unquestionably one of the oddest words in the entire New Testament. Why is it so odd? Because it is a compound word of the word *di*, meaning two, and the word *stomos*, which is the Greek word for one's *mouth*. Thus, when these two words are compounded into one (*distomos*), they describe something that is *two-mouthed*! Don't you agree that this seems a little strange? So why would the Bible refer to the Word of God repeatedly as a 'two-edged sword' or literally, a '*two-mouthed sword*'?

"The Word of God is like a sword that has two edges, cutting both ways and doing terrible damage to an aggressor. Ephesians 6:17 calls it *'the sword of the Spirit, which is the word of God.'* The term, *word*, is taken from the Greek word *rhema*, which describes 'something that is spoken clearly, vividly, in unmistakable terms and undeniable language.' In the New Testament, the word *rhema* carries the idea of a *quickened word*.

"Here is an example of a *rhema* or a *quickened word*: You are praying about a situation, and suddenly a Bible verse rises up from inside your heart. At that moment, you are consciously aware that God has given you a verse to stand on and to claim for your situation. You have received a word that came right *out of the mouth of God* and dropped into your spirit! That word was so sharp that it cut right through your questions, intellect, and natural logic and lodged deep within your heart.

"After you meditate on that *rhema*, or that quickened word from God, it suddenly began to release its power inside you. Soon you could not contain it any longer! Everything within you wanted to *declare* what God had said to you. You wanted to say it. You wanted to release it *out of your mouth*! And when you did, those powerful words were sent forth like a mighty blade to drive back the forces of hell that had marshaled against you, your family, your business, your ministry, your finances, your relationship, or your body. "First, that word came out of the mouth of God. Next, it came out of your mouth! When it came out of *your* mouth, it became a sharp, 'two-edged'—or literally, a 'two-mouthed'—sword. One edge of this sword came into existence when the Word initially proceeded *out of God's mouth*. The second edge of this sword was added when the Word of God proceeded *out of* YOUR *mouth*!

"The Word of God remains a one-bladed sword when it comes out of the God's mouth and drops into your heart but is never released from your own mouth by faith. That supernatural word simple lies dormant in your heart, never becoming the two-edged sword God designed it to be.

"But something happens in the realm of the Spirit when you finally rise up and begin to speak forth that word. The moment it

217

comes out of your mouth, a second edge is added to the blade! Nothing is more powerful than a word that comes first from God's mouth and then from your mouth. You and God have come into agreement, and that agreement releases His mighty power into the situation at hand!"

So yes, God is so good that He confirms His Word to us, so good that He leads us by His Spirit into all truth. It is God's desire to equip us with His principles that will cause us to triumph in life.

Coming back to my journey, there was something trying to suck the very life out of me. The truth of God's Word was giving me an assurance, a hope, that God was on my side and that He was working on my behalf. I knew if He delivered others, He would do it for me too. He is not a respecter of persons, and He never goes back on His Word.

Time has come and gone on this journey. It has been eleven years now. I have to say: I know where I once was, and I know where I am now. Although there is a little that still needs to be dealt with, I am nowhere near where I once was. I read more now than I ever have. My brain is functioning so much better. And I am still thanking God for the completion of the little that is trying to hold on.

I am excited to end this book with twelve chapters. I didn't think I would get that far. That is exciting because the number 12 means perfect government. I like how Daddy God has a sense of humor. Yes, Daddy has a perfect government, and yes, He has a judicial system that He Himself upholds. He is the One who has been leading me to study His courts in Heaven. He is in control, and this is a witness to His perfect plan. But what I am really excited about is that I have ten recorded chapters of ten encounters.

Holy Spirit led me on a journey with the number 10 and 1010 as well. He randomly led me to look at clocks, billboards, you name it. These numbers would repeat themselves in so many ways.

In my spirit, I was reminded of John 10:10:

The thief cometh not, but for to steal, and to kill, and to destroy: I am come that they might have life, and that they might have it more abundantly. (KJV)

I later learned that 10 meant divine order. God brings divine order back into our lives. I could go on and on with other numbers that He has made me aware of, but that is for another time.

This is Daddy's way of speaking to me, letting me know that He is bringing divine order back into my health, and with that divine order comes revelation.

I said all that to say this: Up until the present, I was have never been given an actual diagnosis, but in early January of 2022, I had a dream. It seemed that I was in a salon getting my hair done. The stylist was combing through my hair, separating it as they do, when suddenly, she wanted to say something but was very hesitant. I knew something was not right. I then heard her say, "Miss Emelda, your head ... , your head is full of ticks. They're everywhere."

In my dream, I was appalled. I was embarrassed and said, "Oh no, not me! I don't have lice in my head." But it was not lice that were attached to my scalp. They were ticks. Then I woke up.

Of course, I was disturbed by this dream. Who wants to be known as having lice in their hair, even if it was in a dream? As you can see, I continued to call them lice, although they were ticks. By the way, I had a hair appointment later that very same day. What are the odds of that?

Early that morning, I was working on my old laptop (even though I had a brand-new one). The laptop extended about an inch off the table. When I went to reposition myself, my robe lifted the edge of laptop up a little, and it fell hard on the table. In that moment, everything went dark. "Oh, no! All that work I had just put into it. Noooo, I just can't lose all of that."

This, besides everything else that was still stored on this old laptop and had not yet been transferred to my new one. With time running out on me, I knew I needed to shut down what I was doing anyway. I laid my hands on that laptop and prayed over it that it would reboot in Jesus' name. I could not afford to lose all that I had done. With that, I closed my laptop and went to take a shower.

While in the shower washing my hair, I was reminded of the dream I had during the night. As I was washing my hair, the dream unfolded, and the meaning of it came forth in the spiritual realm. There was a picture before me revealing that TICKS HAD BEEN SUCKING ON MY HEAD, PENETRATING INTO MY BRAIN, AND THEY WERE SUCKING THE VERY LIFE OUT OF ME. That was the problem of my health issues. Wow! Right away I began to pray, thanking God for revealing to me what had been going on. I began binding this phenomenon and releasing it off of me in Jesus' name. I slipped into a Holy Ghost prayer. Then, within minutes, I got a download that my brain was getting rebooted just like my laptop was getting rebooted in my room. I began laughing and laughing and laughing some more. It was amazing.

After I got dressed, I queried Google, "What is a tick on the brain?" and this is what came up:

> Powassan is a rare tick-borne disease caused by a virus. It can cause swelling in the brain. It causes lyme disease. It attacks the nervous system, affecting memory, thinking and balance.

I'm not saying that I had lyme disease, but I was coming to an understanding that this was an attack against my brain in the spiritual realm. And it just so happened that everything I went through mimicked that disease. How interesting to know that multiple sclerosis also mimics lyme disease. I guess that was why my neurologist felt he was spot on from the beginning, thinking I had MS. But my test results didn't agree, so he couldn't diagnosis it as MS.

Coming back to the morning after my dream and the revealing of the tick meaning:

I went back to check on my old laptop, and there on the screen in huge letters were two words to the effect "TO RECONFIGURE." I pressed on the laptop and it began to re-boot. What a miracle that was! Later, to my surprise, this old laptop had taken a complete charge. For some time, it had stopped doing that, but now it showed fully charged. It, too, was miraculously healed.

The conclusion of my tenth encounter ends this way:

Holy Spirit revealed this unaware encounter, leading me straight into the dimension of the courts where my Daddy presides over the Throne of Grace. This was the part of my story that had not existed to my knowledge. This was the gem of the opening of my story. In my opening chapters, I explained that we can come before the Throne of Grace, which is in the courts of Heaven. We approach this Throne when we have a need as seen in the Scriptures.

When I first cried out to Daddy in my kitchen, I said, "God, I cannot do this anymore." You may not have noticed, but I didn't acknowledge Him as Daddy in that moment, as I usually had done. My cry was not looking for help. Apparently, in that moment, my flesh felt abandoned by Him, but my spirit within me knew better. Although I had not addressed Him as my Daddy, the One I could go to for help, He didn't forget who He was to me.

Little did I know in those moments, but I was actually pleading my case before Him. My voice had penetrated straight into the courts of Heaven, and it had caught the attention of Daddy, who sits on His Throne of Grace, and He answered my uneducated petition, as I lay for dead there on the kitchen floor.

Yes, Daddy came to my rescue and He began meeting my needs as He heard me from His court. His Word proclaims His love for us, as we see in the Scriptures. This was truly where my story began, even though I failed to see it as such. My journey to Midbar was the story inside of my story with the courts of Heaven. How glorious is all that!

Let us therefore come boldly to the throne of grace, that we may obtain mercy and find grace to help in time of need. Hebrews 4:16, NKJV

He [Jesus] said to them, "When you pray, say:

226

"Father,
hallowed be your name,
your kingdom come.
Give us each day our daily bread."
Luke 11:2-3

At a glance, we may focus on food as our daily need. However, *"give us each day our daily bread"* is also in reference to meeting all our needs. We have many, and it is the Father's joy to give us what we need.

I had a need that only my Daddy could take care of. It was met in the Throne Room of Grace where He presides when I came boldly into His courts, although, at that moment, I didn't perceive of myself as being there. He not only met my physical need for healing; what He did was so much more than that. He brought me to a beautiful place way beyond anything I could have imagined. He brought me into a deeper intimate relationship with Himself. One thing I know: some way, somehow, Daddy took what the enemy meant for harm and turned it around for His (and my) good

Looking back, I can see Psalm 32:7-8 was my covering, and I will paraphrase:

Daddy was my hiding place. He did protect me from trouble, and He did surround me with songs of deliverance. He did instruct me and taught me in the way I should go. He did counsel me with His loving eyes as He looked upon me.

Looking back at the post of Gretchen Mure Rodriguez, I, too, have adopted this saying for myself because I lived in Midbar, I lived in the wilderness. I am very aware of this place and all it has to offer. This is reality to me and I am so thankful, ever so grateful for the year and a half that I dwelled there. Truly without hesitation, I can proclaim:

"THE WILDERNESS THAT STRIPPED ME BARE, BECAME MY BEAUTIFUL VICTORY!"

Way before time, Jesus wrote a book about me in Heaven. My name is on it. This book contains all the thoughts Jesus had concerning me, all the plans and purposes He desired for me.

I believe that what I have been through was not a part of His plan. Even though in the midst of it all, He made all things new. He restored me and my life on earth still reflects the goodness of God. My book, my life ends well! Jesus is the Author and the Finisher of my faith.

On January 18, 2020, Holy Spirit revealed this truth concerning my life here on earth. It was given to Him out of the goodness of my Daddy. He wanted me to know this and these were the words He spoke to me:

I AM MERELY WORDS GOD WROTE ABOUT BEFORE TIME, AND MY FLESH IS MY BINDER!

What I want to say is this, "To God be the glory for all that He has done for me, for where He has brought me from, and where

He is leading me to and for loving me. I know that the work He has started in me He will finish for His glory."

Amen!

Notes

CHAPTER 2: HEAVEN AND EARTH, MIRROR IMAGE

1. Elizabeth A. Nixon, Esq., Whitequillmedia.com – page 35 *The Courts of Heaven*, 2017
2. Joshua Mills, www.joshuamills.com – page 42. *Activating Angles In Your Life*, *Angelic Activations & Heavenly Encounters* 2-CD Set 2019
3. Christin @garmentsofsplendor.com – page 44 *Garments of Splendor, Covered by Grace, Clothed in Freedom*
4. *Merriam-Webster Dictionary* – Acquitted –page 49
5. Thesaurus - Acquit – page 49
6. God – page 49 *Bible Tool Greek/Hebrew Definitions Strong's Concordance* #2316: *Theos Thayer's Greek Lexicon:* 4a1 – "Magistrate or Divine Judge," James 4:12 (KJV), Psalm 7:11 (KJV)
7. JUDGE - page 51 *Bible Tool Greek/Hebrew Definitions Strong's Concordance* #8199: *shaphat* – "to Judge, to Govern. *Brown-Driver-Briggs Hebrew Lexicon:* "1) to judge, govern, vindicate -- punish 1a2) to decide controversy (of God, man)" Hebrews 12:22-24 (NIV), Luke 18:1-8 (NIV)
8. LAWGIVER -page 52 *Strong's Concordance* #3550: *Nomothetes* – "a lawgiver." *Strong's Hebrew* #2710: *chaqaq* Outline of Bible Usage: "2. One who decrees, lawgiver" Isaiah 33:22 (KJV)
9. JESUS – "Mediator/Arbitrator" – page 53 Biblehub.com *Strong's Greek* #3315: *mesiteuo* – "to interpose, mediate" *Thayer's Greek Lexicon:* "1) to **act as a mediator** between litigating or covenanting parties. 1a) to accomplish something between two parties" *Strong's Exhaustive Concordance* – from *mesites,* "to interpose (as arbiter)"
10. JESUS – "Advocate/Defense Lawyer/Attorney" – page 53 *Bible Tool Greek/Hebrew Definitions Strong's Concordance* #3875: *parakletos* - "an intercessor, consoler:--**advocate**, comforter" *Thayer's Greek Lexicon:* "1)summoned, called to one's side, especially called to one's aid 1a) one who pleads another's cause before a judge, a pleader, counsel for defense, legal assistant, an advocate (page 54) 1b1) of Christ in His

exaltation at God's right hand, pleading with God the Father for the pardon of our sins."

11. Satan – "The Prosecuting Attorney" (page 54) **"Accuser"** - *Bible Tool Greek/Hebrew Strong's Concordance* #2723: *kategoreo* – from 2725; "to be a plaintiff, i.e. to charge with some offense:-accuse, object" *Thayer's Greek Lexicon*: "1) to accuse 1a) before a judge to make an accusation 1b) of an extrajudicial accusation" *Liddell-Scott-Jones Definitions*: "accuser, public prosecutor" (page 55)

12. Adversary – (page 56) *Bible Tool Greek* #476: *antidikos* — from 473 and 1349; **"an opponent (in a lawsuit)**; specially, Satan (as the arch-enemy): adversary"

13. Petitions – (page 56) *Bible Tool Greek/Hebrew Definitions Strong's Concordance* #7596: *shelah*, "a petition, request" *Brown-Driver-Briggs Hebrew Lexicon*: "1) request, thing asked for, demand 1a) request, petition"

14. Persecutors – (page 58) Psalm 3:1 (KJV)

15. Verdict- (page 58) Proverbs 16:10 **(NAS)**

16. Sentence – (page 58) Luke 23:24 (KJV)

CHAPTER 6: STANDING IN PROXY, PROXY

(Page 112) *Merriam-Webster Dictionary* – "a person who is given the power or authority to do something for someone else" (page 113)

CHAPTER 7: A JUST JUDGE

1. One Way Tract – (page 41) Chick Publications, ISBN 978-0-7589-0057-9 www.chick.com 1984-2022

CHAPTER 8: PRAYER ROOM THRONE ROOM

1. "War Room" – (page 131) release date August 28, 2015 by Sony Pictures

2. Dwell – (page 138) *Bible Tool Greek/Hebrew Definitions Strong's Concordance* #3427: *yashab* "to sit down, to remain, to settle, to marry: to abide, habitation, make to keep house, marry"

3. "Eternity Swallowed Up Time" Joshua Mills – (page 142) Glory Bible Study, aired on August 24, 2022

Notes

CHAPTER 9: ORDER IN THE COURT

1. *The Not-So-Silent Night*: Instant Christmas Pageant (Just add Kids) (page 143) Group Publishing, Published Date 07/21/15 Item#: 9781470732738

CHAPTER 10: SYMPHONY OF HEAVEN_

1. Steve Swanson 2015 – Heaven's Symphony – (page 58) Destiny Image ISBN 13: 978-0-7684-0539-2

CHAPTER 12: THRONE OF GRACE

1. Dwell – (page 189) *Bible Tool Greek/Hebrew Definitions Strong's Concordance* #3427: *yashab*, "to sit down, to remain, to settle, to marry: to abide, habitation, make to keep house, marry" (page 190)

2. Mary Ellen Wright – *Hear God's Heart – Treasures from Psalm 91:1* maryellenwrights.com August 31, 2015

3. Abide – (page 191) *Bible Tools Strong's Greek Concordance* #3306: *meno* "to stay (in a given place, state, relation or expectancy): abide, continue, dwell, endure, be present, remain, stand, tarry (for)" *Biblehub. com Strong's Concordance* #3885 *luwn*, "to lodge, pass the night, abide"

4. *The Prayer of Protection: Living Fearlessly in Dangerous Times* by Joseph Prince (page 193)

5. Midbar – (page 196) *Bible Tool Greek/Hebrew Definitions Strong's Concordance* #4057: *midbar*, "speech, wilderness" *Brown-Driver-Briggs Lexicon:* "1) Wilderness 2) Mouth 2a) Mouth (as organ of speech). *Biblehub.com NAS Exhaustive Concordance* – #4057 a *midbar*, word origin from *dabar (page 197)* – Definition - "mouth" *Biblehub.com NAS Exhaustive Concordance* - #4057b *midbar*, word origin from *dabar* – "wilderness"
Dabar - *Bible Tool Greek/Hebrew Definitions Strong's Concordance* #1696: *dabar*, "words, to speak"

6. Photini – (page 200) Antiochian Orthodox Christian Archdiocese

7. Gretchen Mure Rodriguez – (page 206) Quote from Gretch Mure Rodriguez (page 76) "The Wilderness That Stripped Me Bare Became My Beautiful Victory," a post from Facebook (page 207)

8. Rick Renner – article "You Have a Two-Edge Sword" February 21, 2017 (page 213)

9. Psalm 32:7-8 Paraphrased (page 228)

Author Contact Page

You may contact Emelda Menge Williams directly in the following way/s:

Facebook: Emelda Menge Williams

Email: emeldapw@aol.com

Printed in the USA
CPSIA information can be obtained
at www.ICGtesting.com
CBHW031428101223
2394CB00009B/6